Church of God in Christ: Leadership Guidebook for Ministers

Church of God in Christ: Leadership Guidebook for Ministers

Rev. Thomas Jackson Jr.

Copyright © 2010 by Rev. Thomas Jackson Jr.

Library of Congress Control Number:		2009911661
ISBN:	Hardcover	978-1-4415-9568-3
	Softcover	978-1-4415-9567-6

All rights reserved. No part of this book may be reproduced or transmitted in any form or by any means, electronic or mechanical, including photocopying, recording, or by any information storage and retrieval system, without permission in writing from the copyright owner.

This book was printed in the United States of America.

To order additional copies of this book, contact:
Xlibris Corporation
1-888-795-4274
www.Xlibris.com
Orders@Xlibris.com
69276

CONTENTS

PREFACE vii
ACKNOWLEDGMENTS ix
INTRODUCTION 1
GUIDEBOOK OUTLINE 3

I. GENERAL INFORMATION, CHURCH OF GOD IN CHRIST 7
    A.   CONSTITUTION OVERVIEW 7
        1.   Church of God in Christ Electoral Flowchart 10
        2.   The Election Process in the Church of God in Christ 12
        3.   Church of God in Christ Legislative Branch 13
        4.   Church of God in Christ Executive Branch 14
        5.   Church of God in Christ Judicial Branch 15
        6.   Church of God in Christ Inc. National Organization Structure 16
    B.   DOCTRINE 17

II. PSYCHOLOGICAL AND MORAL ASPECTS OF THE MINISTRY 18
    A.   IMPORTANCE OF PREACHING 18
    B.   PSYCHOLOGICAL ASPECTS 19
    C.   IMPORTANCE OF PASTORAL OFFICE 20

III. ATTRIBUTES OF A GOOD LEADER 24
    A.   SPIRITUALITY 24
    B.   WHAT IS CHARACTER? 25

IV. OBSTACLES TO PASTORAL GROWTH 31

V. ORGANIZING A NEW CHURCH 32

APPENDICES

APPENDIX 1—DOCTRINES OF THE CHURCH OF GOD IN
   CHRIST 37
APPENDIX 2—CONTRASTS OF SOCIAL AND PASTORAL
   CONVERSATION 43
APPENDIX 3—TEN KEYS TO LEADERSHIP 44
APPENDIX 4—FACTORS IN NONVERBAL COMMUNICATION 45
APPENDIX 5—BEHAVIOR THAT CAN ENCOURAGE ACTIVE
   LISTENING 47
APPENDIX 6—WHAT IS PARLIAMENTARY LAW? 49
APPENDIX 7—WRITING AND IMPLEMENTING THE VISION 58

HANDOUT 1— SUPERINTENDENT'S JOB OVERVIEW 63
HANDOUT 2— FIRST JURISDICTION—ILLINOIS
   EXECUTIVE LEADERSHIP INSTITUTE 65
HANDOUT 3— FIRST JURISDICTION—ILLINOIS 66
HANDOUT 4— THE JURISDICTIONAL BUDGET MANUAL 94
HANDOUT 5— JUDICIARY BOARD 138
HANDOUT 6— FOUR-STEP PROBLEM-SOLVING APPROACH 152
HANDOUT 7— PROCEDURES FOR CONDUCTING A
   JURISDICTIONAL TRIAL 153
HANDOUT 8— COULD YOU JUST LISTEN 159
HANDOUT 9— ORGANIZING A NEW CHURCH 161

INDEX 163

PREFACE

THIS GUIDEBOOK IS for church leaders who are seeking methods and approaches that will be effective in the growth of their ministries. It is devoted exclusively to ministerial leadership issues and will provide insights into important areas facing churchmen today.

The scriptures show that the purpose, activity, and concern of the early Christian leaders were always that the church may grow. There is an obvious need for the same attitude, spirit, and commitment today. Our goal is to build that kind of ministry that will help us to come to grips with the task of strengthening each other.

Complacency and unwillingness to give unselfishly of time and abilities have dried up evangelism and, consequently, the conversion growth of the church. Negativism and a defeatist attitude have no place in the church.

A final word should be said concerning some guiding principles that the editor has attempted to follow throughout the process of developing this work. Nobody can fully please everybody—we have tried to design a balanced book of interest and value to church leaders generally. Our hope is that the material will provide information that will expand the reader's vision and concern beyond his own immediate need, thereby enriching the ministry.

Rev. Thomas Jackson Jr
Chicago, Illinois

ACKNOWLEDGMENTS

THE EDITOR WISHES to express deep gratitude to all authors and publications whose works were made available for inclusion in this guidebook. These include the Holy Bible, *A Handbook for the Preachers at Work* by Jeff D. Brown, *The Mystery of Preaching* by James Black, *Men Who Build Churches* by Harold A. Bosley, and *Character* by D. Starke. Special acknowledgment and deep appreciation for the assistance given goes to Ms. Janis McReynolds, who assembled with great resourcefulness the data and materials in this publication.

Finally, the editor wishes to acknowledge and appreciate a number of ministerial colleagues and friends who encouraged the undertaking and provided many helpful suggestions to him. To all of these, the editor extends his thanks.

INTRODUCTION

PSYCHOLOGICAL AND MORAL ASPECTS OF THE MINISTRY

THERE IS A crisis in the black community, and angry voices are crying for positive leadership. The massive and growing concentration of impoverished blacks has caused a greatly increased burden on the depleted resources of the city. This has created a growing crisis of deteriorating facilities and services and unmet human needs.

More often than not, "black ghetto" has meant segregation, poverty, no opportunity, enforced failure, split families, self-denigration, bitterness and resentment against society in general and white society in particular.

One of the more obvious dilemmas is the lack of positive male role identification and male responsibility in community problem solving.

The 1990s were paradoxical, a time of great blessing for the church, also a time of increased drug activity, gang warfare, unemployment, murders, and general moral deterioration among many of our communities. These problems, just as our blessings, are continuing in an upswing. There is also a crisis among our youth, and angry voices are crying out for positive leadership. Spiritual denigration has caused concern throughout the country—*the ministers must make a difference!*

The church, in its ecumenical form, is one of the oldest and most respected institutions in the country. Together we have the knowledge, the wisdom, and, most of all, the spiritual presence to be a great influence in our communities and in the lives of our people.

We cannot let such a great opportunity pass us by! Let us seize the moment!

Just as the 1990s proved to be the most morally degenerate and chaotic decade in our history, it also provided the best opportunity for us, as leaders, to make a profound difference—naturally and spiritually. No one works harder at understanding the needs of our people than we do.

The twenty-first century is our challenge!

GUIDEBOOK OUTLINE

I. GENERAL INFORMATION, CHURCH OF GOD IN CHRIST
   A. Constitution Overview
   B. Doctrine
      1. Articles of Religion
      2. Ordinances—Communion, Feet Washing, Funerals, Marriage

II. PSYCHOLOGICAL AND MORAL ASPECTS OF THE MINISTRY
   A. Importance of Preaching
      1. Audience
      2. Message
      3. Preacher

   B. Psychological Aspects
      1. Attitude toward Self and Congregation
      2. Quality of Relationship with God

   C. Importance of Pastoral Office
      1. Tragedy of Failure
      2. Measuring Success

   D. Four Moral Requirements
      1. Bondable Word
      2. Ability to Unify
      3. Discipline in Life and Thought
      4. Courage to Face the Crucial Issues

III. ATTRIBUTES OF A GOOD LEADER
   A. Spirituality
   B. Character
      1. Elements of a Good Character
      2. What Can Your Character Achieve?
      3. How Can One Develop Good Character?

   C. Attitude
      1. Financial Needs
      2. Socialization
      3. Tentative Results
      4. Competition
      5. Meditation

IV. OBSTACLES TO MINISTERIAL GROWTH
   A. Seven Deadly Sins
- Pride
- Envy
- Covetousness
- Anger
- Lust
- Sloth
- Gluttony

   B. Other Distractions
      1. Personal Anxieties
      2. Pastoral Cowardice
      3. Constant Tension

V. ORGANIZING A CHURCH
  A. Organizing/Personnel and Staff Requirements
    1. Corporate Charter, Constitution, Bylaws
    2. Site and Facility, Insurance
    3. IRS Compliance and Tax Exemptions
  B. Spiritual Ministry
     - Worship
     - Education
     - Fellowship
     - Ministry Plan

I

GENERAL INFORMATION, CHURCH OF GOD IN CHRIST

A. CONSTITUTION OVERVIEW

THE FOLLOWING INFORMATION is not being given to reflect the entire history of the Church of God in Christ, but to review the legal framework of government established by constitution and resolution.

Formally, the present Church of God in Christ's constitution, adopted in 1922 and amended several times since, divides the church government into three branches. The legislative branch determines what the laws shall be, the executive branch executes or administers the law, and the judicial branch construes and applies the law.

On December 18, 1921, the Church of God in Christ Inc. was incorporated or qualified to do business in the state of Tennessee. The incorporated name was the General Board of the Church of God in Christ of America. The twelve incorporators constituted the first board of directors and were given the authority to elect a president, a secretary, and a treasurer. They were further given "the power to increase the number of directors from twelve to thirty-six, provided, however, the same be ordered by resolution of the General Convocation of the Church of God in Christ."

On December 31, 1926, an amendment to the charter was filed with the Tennessee secretary of state to change the name from "the General Board of the Church of God in Christ of America" to "Church of God in Christ." Other modifications included the codifying of the charter into articles that defined the principles of faith and government with the following specific restrictions on the general assembly:

1. It shall not set aside or change any of our articles of faith, nor shall it establish any new doctrines contrary to the doctrines that now exist in the church.
2. The general assembly shall not abolish our representative form of government or the general superintendency or deprive it of any of the power given it by this constitution.
3. The general assembly shall not deprive our ministers or members of a fair and orderly trial or an appeal in case of conviction.

On January 10, 1927, an amendment to the charter was filed with the Tennessee secretary of state to change provisions of articles 3, 4, 5, and 6, which had to do with organization of local churches and the credentials of delegates to the general assembly.

On December 5, 1952, an amendment to the charter was filed with the Tennessee secretary of state to change provisions of articles 1-5, 7, and 10-18, which had to do with the following modifications: changes of address of the headquarters; the organization of local churches; rules of order of the general assembly; power of overseers of the Church of God in Christ; powers of the board of bishops; organization of Women's Department and other departments; trustees of local churches; trials of local churches and officials; eligibility of elders; trials of elders, overseers, and bishops.

On November 17, 1961, the founder and chief apostle passed away. Afterward, a controversy developed "with respect to where the authority and leadership of the Church of God in Christ" was placed by the 1952 amendment to the constitution.

Pursuant to a consent decree entered in Shelby County Chancery Court, Tennessee, on October 29, 1967, and as the result of a constitutional convention convened pursuant to a settlement decree, an effort was made to resolve the controversy and update the Church of God in Christ constitution.

On February 23, 1968, an amendment to the charter was filed with the Tennessee secretary of state to place authority of doctrine-expressing and law-making of the church under the general assembly . . . established an election process for the election of a twelve-man general board, a presiding bishop, and a first and second assistant presiding bishop who "would be empowered to conduct the executive affairs of the Church of God in Christ between meetings of the general Assembly and the General Board, with the limitation that the action of the Presiding Bishop would be subject to the approval of a majority of the General Board and the General Assembly" and also abolished the office of senior bishop and executive board of bishops.

On October 30, 1972, an amendment to the charter was filed with the Tennessee secretary of state to make major modifications, including the following: a declaration of faith and preamble, a name change from "Church of God in Christ" to "Church of God in Christ Inc.," changes in the civil and ecclesiastical structure of the church, including duties, election, and terms. This was the last major amendment filed with the Tennessee secretary of state. However, much legislation has occurred since October 30, 1971. This manuscript will incorporate any changes that have been made insofar as it affects the electoral process in the Church of God in Christ.

On September 16, 2003, a constitutional convention was held in St. Louis, Missouri. Many recommendations for amendments to the Church of God in Christ were offered. They are being reviewed and studied by the general assembly.

1. # CHURCH OF GOD IN CHRIST ELECTORAL FLOWCHART

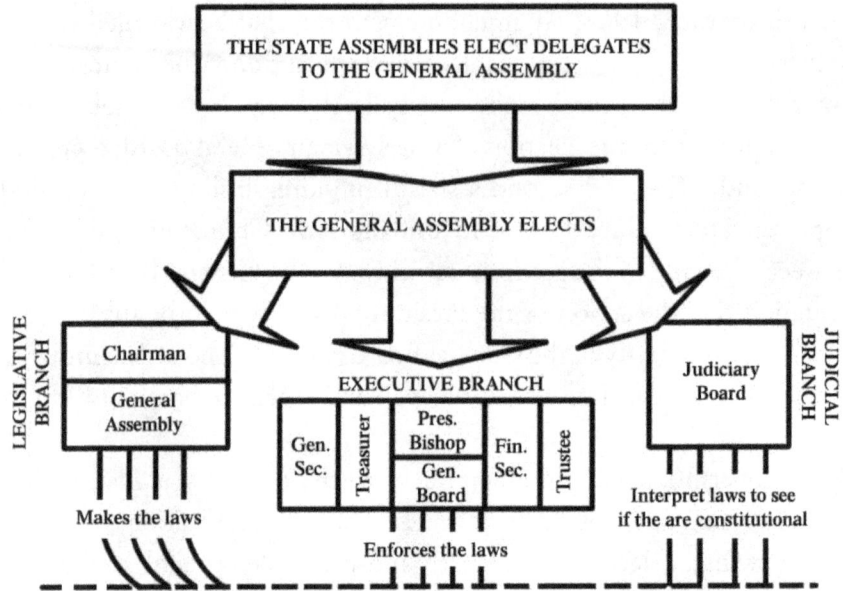

The amended constitution provides for three branches in the government of the church: the legislative, the executive, and the judicial.

The legislative branch is composed of a general assembly headed by its chairman, consisting of qualified elected delegates from the state jurisdictions. The general assembly is the supreme legislative authority of the Church of God in Christ. It is the only tribunal that has power to express the doctrines and creeds of the church.

The presiding bishop is the head of the executive branch and is the chief executive officer of the Church of God in Christ. He presides over all sessions of the general board and has the power and authority to conduct the executive functions of the church when neither the general board nor the general assembly is in session. All executive branch officers are elected by the general assembly.

The judicial branch of the church is composed of a judiciary board (supreme court) and other judicial courts. These men, learned in church law, are to deal especially with disputes about the meaning of the constitution. They are also to settle disputes as the final ecclesiastical and appellate court within the Church of God in Christ. They are elected by the general assembly.

2. THE ELECTION PROCESS IN THE CHURCH OF GOD IN CHRIST

The election process is one of the most valuable rights and duties that a delegate of the Church of God in Christ general assembly has. To neglect his or her obligation to the election process is, in effect, to neglect his or her birthright. Whatever is good or bad in the church's legislative and administrative life is a direct reaction to the actions, or lack of actions, on the part of the voter.

To be a qualified delegate of the general assembly, a person must be certified by the general secretary in one of the following categories:

1. Member of the general board
2. Jurisdictional bishop
3. Jurisdictional supervisor of women's work
4. Pastors of local churches
5. Ordained elder
6. District missionary
7. Layman
8. Foreign delegate
9. Children of the founder

The constitution carefully governs the requirements for certification.

As we minister in the twenty-first century, the Church of God in Christ is taking its rightful place as the leader confronting a future that will offer unprecedented challenges. We, as leaders, now have the best opportunity to make a profound difference, naturally and spiritually. The election of competent, spirit-filled, godly men and women to positions of authority and responsibilities in the church should take priority as each candidate presents himself for consideration. To this end, efforts made in this guidebook are designed to help the participants understand *the importance of an informed electorate.*

3. CHURCH OF GOD IN CHRIST LEGISLATIVE BRANCH

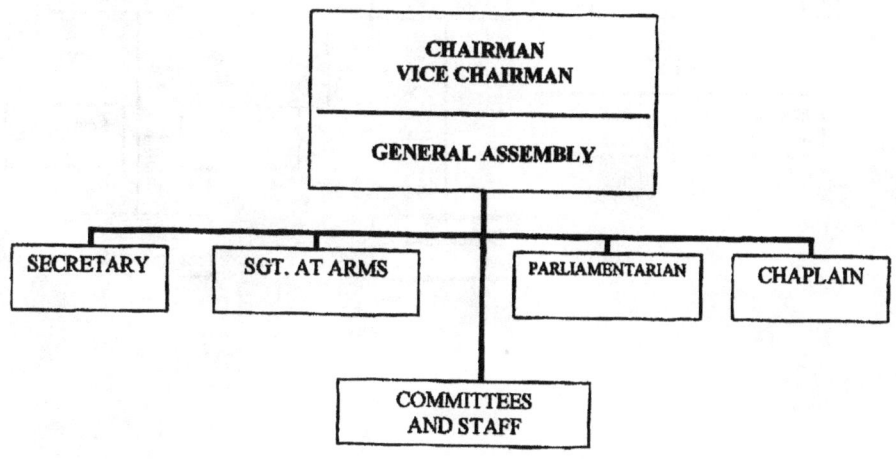

4. CHURCH OF GOD IN CHRIST EXECUTIVE BRANCH

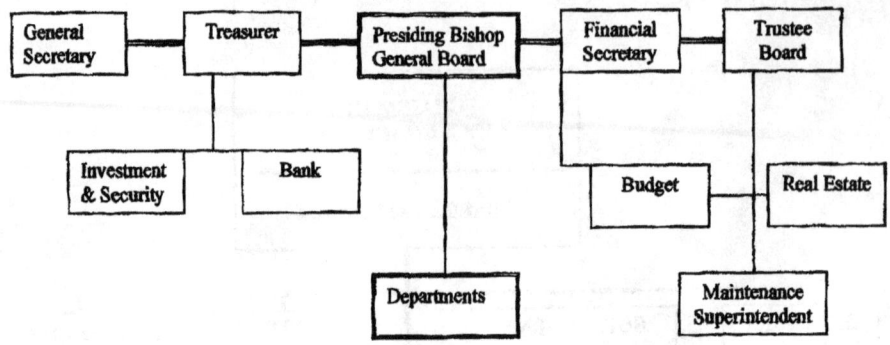

5. CHURCH OF GOD IN CHRIST JUDICIAL BRANCH

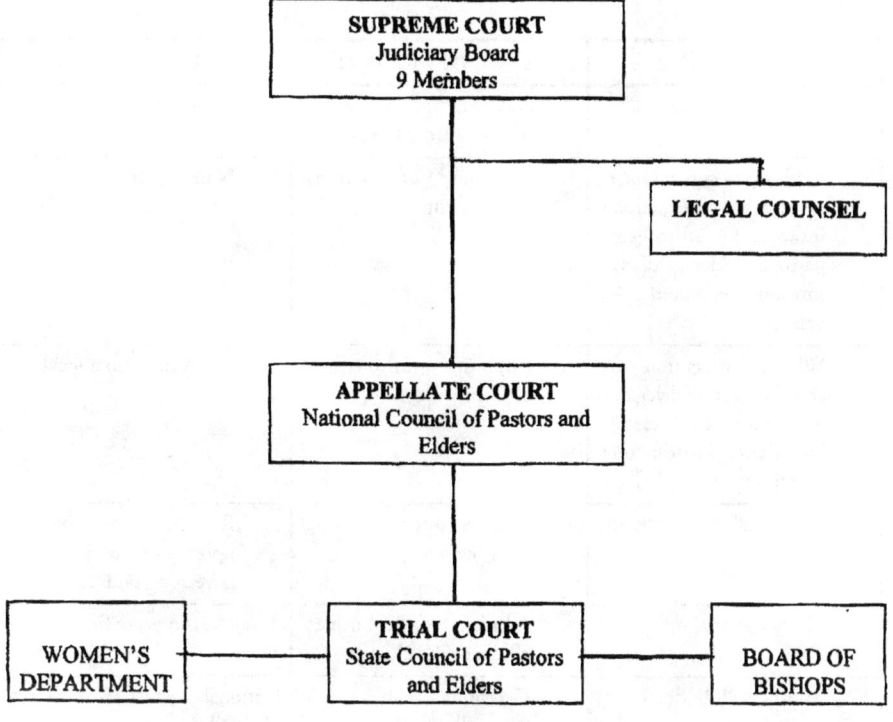

6. CHURCH OF GOD IN CHRIST INC. NATIONAL ORGANIZATION STRUCTURE

LEGISLATIVE	ADMINISTRATIVE	JUDICIAL
General Assembly	Presiding Bishop and General Board (12)	Judiciary Board
1. Made up of general board members, jurisdictional bishops, supervisors, pastors, elders, district missionaries, and lay delegates	1. Appoints head of national departments	1. Nine (9) members elected by the general assembly
2. With the exception of a certain class of delegates, delegates are elected by their jurisdictional assembly	2. Appoints jurisdictional bishops	2. Hears cases on appeal
3. Makes all laws for the church	3. Presides over the national convocation	3. Renders legal opinions upon request by other governing bodies
4. Elects national officers	4. Administers the business affairs of the church	4. Decisions are final
5. Approves all budgets	5. Decisions subject to the will of the general assembly	National Pastors' and Elders' Council 1. All pastors and elders 2. Is an appeals court 3. Decisions are implemented by jurisdictional bishops

ECCLESIASTICAL
General assembly
General board
Judiciary board
Board of bishops
General council
Women's Department
Jurisdictional assemblies
Local churches

B. DOCTRINE

1. ARTICLES OF RELIGION
   - Doctrine of the Church of God in Christ
     (Statement of Faith—A Brief Summary) Appendix 1

2. Ordinances of the Church of God in Christ (the Sacraments)
   - A *sacrament*, as commonly defined, is "an outward and visible sign setting forth and pledging an inward, invisible grace." In the sacraments, the primacy of grace is emphasized. It is God who, first of all, does something. In these observances, he comes to assure us that his promises are true and that they are being individualized.
   - The Lord's Supper (Communion)
     i. It is a *memorial* to the death of Christ for the sins of the world.
     ii. It signifies *thanksgiving*. As saints, we offer unto God our thanksgiving and praise for what Christ accomplished in our behalf.
     iii. It represents fellowship—we experience spiritual union with Christ, one another, and other saints on earth.
     iv. It stands for sacrifice. In the light of atonement, man offers himself as a living sacrifice to God.
   - Baptism—baptism dispensed following repentance was a symbol of cleansing from sin and consecration to the way of Christ.
   - Feet washing—demonstrates that humility characterized greatness in the Kingdom.

II

PSYCHOLOGICAL AND MORAL ASPECTS OF THE MINISTRY

A. IMPORTANCE OF PREACHING

1. Audience
   - Listening to people prescribes the form, tone, and color of preaching. The message must relate to people.

2. Message
   - Preach the truth (it is the truth that heals, and it is healing that men need).
   - Preach what you believe (faith)—not pet theories or views.
   - Preach for results—you want to convince men and lead them to Christ.

3. Preacher
   - Your personality (your personal touch)—you have a distinctive point of view and distinctive characteristics.
   - Never imitate.
   - Acknowledge resources.
   - Be bold with the course of conviction—what is the prophetic note?

B. PSYCHOLOGICAL ASPECTS
(Occupational Hazards)

- Bothered by the fact that much of our work is tentative
- Aware of corrosive effects of competition
- A growing tendency to sit in meditation, which is actually laziness and indecision
- May lose sight of goal, trying to satisfy organizational and people's claims
- Attempting to preserve a professional front but building a dual personality

   1. Attitude toward self and congregation
      - People you are leading are not stupid.
      - Difference between a leader and the people.
      - What happens if a leader shows weakness?

   2. What is attitude?
      - Attitude covers one's demeanor in relationship to other people.
      - Attitude is one's expression of his or her innermost feelings that are demonstrated to others.
      - Attitude is one's expression of his or her true self.
      - One's attitude shapes one's character.

C. IMPORTANCE OF PASTORAL OFFICE

When we consider the importance of the pastoral office, we are thinking of the greatest and most important work in the world. God has called and ordained for this specific purpose. God not only calls men to service, but he also provides them with the necessary talent, strength, and wisdom. In calling and endowing them for the purpose of leading his people, he does not leave them to themselves. He becomes their parents.

The pastor is the spiritual example in the community where he lives. He must set the example for Christian living and giving. Everybody watches him and his family. It is important that he keep himself unspotted from the world.

The responsibilities involved in pastoral office are very important:

- Most important is his personal work with the unsaved—personal and winning.
- He is responsible for preaching to every creature. Preaching requires utmost prayer and meditation, careful study and thorough preparation.
- He is responsible for the knowledge of the scriptures the people receive.
- He must not only preach—he must instruct.
- He must visit and comfort the sick and the afflicted.

1. TRAGEDY OF FAILURE

The failure of a pastor is a tragedy. The failure of *one* pastor may be the indirect downfall of *many*. There are many explanations for the failure of a pastor. Failure to consider these and to avoid them is the first step down.

> The man who fails to consider, from the human standpoint, the hardships, the heartaches, the difficulties, and the disadvantages of a pastorate is a failure to begin with.

The pastorate is not an easy way to earn a living. He is constantly in the limelight. All eyes are on him. He is not considered "human" in the common sense of the word; he must be superhuman in his standards, his thinking, and in his living.

Failure in prayer life will contribute to the failure of a pastor. He must pray without ceasing for spiritual guidance and power. He must pray for wisdom. He must pray for the people of his church. He must pray for the lost. Men of old whose education was limited enjoyed a great measure of success because they gave themselves to fervent prayer. Prayer is vitally important in the life of a pastor. He must be a man of prayer.

Many pastors have become failures because they catered to the wrong people. Too many times the most influential people in the community and the church are people who are "worldly-minded." They believe and want a social gospel. They want the pastor to preach from the Bible so long as he doesn't touch them.

When the pastor pampers them and preaches a gospel that does not condemn sin, he has failed God. The pastor must be impartial and seek first to please God.

Many pastors have failed because of sheer laziness. There is no place in the ministry for a lazy preacher.

- Failure to live within his means is another downfall.
- Other things that contribute to failure are

    lack of study and preparation,
    failure in visitation,
    unethical conduct,
    lack of sympathy and compassion,
    lack of vision, and
    arrogance.

In short, the pastor who is not a success is a failure.

2. MEASURING SUCCESS

There are numerous things that contribute to the success of a pastor. I shall list a few. Success is not measured by number; it is measured by faithfulness to God, to the Word, to the church.

It is using God's power to win souls, thereby glorifying Christ.
Success does not come by accident—neither is it hereditary. Success comes by thorough preparedness and hard work.

The most important factor in the minister's success is a divine call from God into the ministry.

Jesus makes men to be soul winners. God prepares the heart of the pastor that he may be spiritually fitted for the high office to which he is called.

Prayer is also important.
Prayer gives the pastor daily strength for the tasks before him.

The individual must be sure of his calling into the ministry.
When the individual is sure of his calling into the ministry, he should prayerfully set himself to the task of preparing himself for this office.

Faithfulness to God and the Bible and the church will bring success.
Faithfulness to God means that when the pastor finds the will of God, he carries out that will no matter what the cost. He will not compromise with the devil or his angels. He will remain true to God in all things. The pastor who is faithful to God is faithful to the Bible—the Word of God. He accepts it, believes in it, and preaches it.

Faithfulness to God and the Bible produces faithfulness of every phase of the church organization.

Vision contributes much to the success of a pastor.
Great churches have been built because a pastor saw possibilities, secured the full cooperation of the congregation, then pressed toward the mark.

III

ATTRIBUTES OF A GOOD LEADER

A. SPIRITUALITY

> ATTRIBUTES OF A GOOD LEADER
> discretion,
> tact,
> patience,
> vision,
> goals,
> understanding,
> intestinal fortitude,
> desire to do a good job
> temperance,
> sincerity,
> positive attitude about self,
> self-confidence,
> discipline,
> commitment,
> etc.

B. WHAT IS CHARACTER?

1. Character is what one is.
2. Reputation is what someone thinks you to be. Character is what you are.
3. Testing one's character
4. The test of one's character is found in the vexations of life, i.e., those problems, troubles, stumbling blocks, actions, or obstacles—those difficulties that will cause us to get into trouble.
5. If you can get through these tests, your character will come out as pure gold.
   - Impulsiveness
   - Impulsive thoughts may lead to impulsive actions. Impulsive actions may get you in trouble. You must control your impulses.
   - Irritability
   - Check irritability. Cultivate calm, which permits you to concentrate on the power that you need to change the storm into calmness. (See appendix 4.)

   Your body has to be brought into harmony with the mind.

   Learn how to actualize patience and perseverance. These help us deal with developing strong character.

6. Elements of a Good Character
   a. Forcefulness of leadership, which is gained by foresight, prudence, discernment, reason, logic, and clear thinking.
   b. Strong character, which requires energy, determination, and a fixed purpose. Foresight, reason, and logic must be practiced for us to develop strong character.
   c. Practice of sound principles (foresight, prudence, discernment, etc.) will allow us to develop mentally, morally, and physically.

      We will be able to rise above difficulties, mount all obstacles, resist temptations, and bear heavy burdens cheerfully.
   d. These will bring calmness to your storm and fearlessness in the face of danger.

> ## DEFINITIONS
>
> Clear thinking—method of thinking (drawing an awareness of certain things). In process of thinking, you utilize logic and reason to arrive at a conclusion. Clear thinking, once we have utilized all of the logic and reasoning we have, is the ability to think through the process using whatever is appropriate at the time.
>
> Logic—common sense, intelligence
>
> Reason—ability to choose proper course, discernment

WHAT CAN CHARACTER ACHIEVE?

Character can accomplish anything.

> Recap: Character is basically what one is—actions and words enable people to react to our true character. These are components of your character, and it is important that you are able to understand this and then move on.
>
> The strength of one's character or what one's character could achieve is based on
>
> *accomplishment* and
> *I* (you, yourself).
> *If* accomplishment *and* I *are tied together, it merely means mastery of yourself.*
>
> This is what character allows us to do. Character is that quality that permits us to choose the things that are within us as we reflect upon the actions that we want to do or accomplish.

HOW DOES ONE'S CHARACTER ACHIEVE?

We must first reflect on what we are all about, reflect on what we want to do.

After having reflected, if we have good character, utilized logic, reasoning, and clear thinking, we are able to look at ourselves, our abilities, our strengths, and our weaknesses and see fit the actions we are going to take are proper and what we need to accomplish them.

At the same time, free yourself or those actions from all foreign occupation. You have to conquer yourself—your own willpower.

One enemy of conquering willpower is fear. Fear is an integral part or the very strong enemy of people who have good character. You should remember two things: you must recognize the need to conquer willpower and strengthen yourself for the attempt.

HOW CAN ONE DEVELOP GOOD CHARACTER?

One must first recognize one's weaknesses and then have the desire for deliverance from those weaknesses.

- Free yourself from superstitions.
- Free yourself from fear.
- Learn to control anger and passion.
- Deliver your mind from the invasion of feeble thoughts (clear the soil).
- Struggle against excessive emotion. Don't give your imagination free rein.

ILLUSTRATION: FARMER SOWING SEEDS

When a farmer plants seeds, before he plants, he goes to the soil and clears the soil of all extraneous material and foreign objects that would keep the seeds from growing (i.e., stones, roots, weeds, everything that would hinder their growth).

Application: You must get your own ground ready. You are the ground. You must clear your own ground from fear and frustrations, confusion, grief, burdens, minds that are in stress, hatred, avarice—all these things are in our field. You have to clear it away.

Once the field is clear of known and obvious extraneous and foreign matter, he further prepares the soil by pulverizing or breaking it up, making it soft enough, fine enough for the seeds to sprout—for its roots and plants to have the least amount of resistance for the seed to come forth and grow.

The farmer will continue to monitor the growth of the plant—not just in terms of watching it to see when the roots come out (this portion is usually hidden from the eye) but also to continue to remove the foreign particles.

Application: The enemy (Satan) will continue to sow seeds and drop foreign matter. Some seeds are good, some bad, but what we want is the seed we planted growing in that spot.

Develop character—master yourself!

MASTERING ONESELF

Before you master your ministry, you must master yourself. Consider the following:

When one has fear, he is not in control of himself. Fear does things that cause one to develop certain imagined things that may or may not be true or proper because he is not applying clear thinking, logic, or reasoning to a specific situation.

Many times the first thoughts that come to our mind in trying situations are incorrect. They give way to our imagination.

You must allow strong character to shine through and clear your mind of extraneous thoughts.

Be prayerful and real positive about what the Lord is doing.

Do not give up hope—there is hope!

As a student of leadership—that is, if your goal is to become a strong leader—you must take the principles discussed in this guidebook and apply them to self to see if you can cooperate with these principles.

Fear is one of the real reasons why people cannot master themselves. Fear affects logic, reasoning, and clear thinking. It infects your common sense, your understanding, your ability to choose the right direction—all of these will be infected by fear, and fear will cause you to lose control.

The following actions must be practiced daily if you are to gain complete control of yourself and your ministries:

- Struggle against excessive emotion. Avoid giving your imagination free rein. If you let everything come into this gate, it will go into your mind and infect it.
- Rid yourself of anger. Anger generally is a built-up thing. It is like a long-term situation.
- Rid yourself of passion. Passion is a fast thing—like a flash fire.
- You can't be a master of your own soul if you allow imagination, anger, and passion to be a part of you.

IV

OBSTACLES TO PASTORAL GROWTH

A. SEVEN DEADLY SINS
  1. Pride
  2. Envy
  3. Covetousness
  4. Anger
  5. Lust
  6. Sloth
  7. Gluttony

B. OTHER DISTRACTIONS
  1. Personal Anxieties
  2. Pastoral Cowardice
  3. Constant Tension

C. PSYCHOLOGICAL SUGGESTIONS THAT HELP
  Persons of Tension

  1. Talk it out.
  2. Escape for a while.
  3. Work off your anger.
  4. Give in occasionally.
  5. Do something for others.
  6. Take one thing at a time.
  7. Shun the "Superman" urge.
  8. Go easy with criticism.
  9. Give the other fellow a break.
  10. Make yourself available.
  11. Schedule your recreation.
  12. If you need help, get an expert.
     (George S. Stevenson, MD, How to Deal with Your Tension)

V

ORGANIZING A NEW CHURCH

ONE IDEA OF *church* in the New Testament, which we shall consider here for this specific purpose, was "a community gathered by God through Christ." The church belongs to God because he has called it into being, dwells within it, rules over it, and realizes his purpose through it.

A real, true church conforms to God's Word; thus, it must follow in doctrine, character, organization, and practice the direction given it by the Bible.

Proverbs 29:18 states, "Where there is no vision, the people perish." Therefore, before organizing a new church, one must seek a vision and direction from God; then, armed with what has been given and divinely inspired by God, a person can proceed with organization. (See appendix 7.)

Procedure in organizing a new church

After praying, meditating, and seeking God's direction for what you believe to be the direction of the Holy Spirit and after receiving the assurance and the vision, the following is a suggested method for getting started:

I. Call a meeting of family, baptized believers, and all that are interested in organizing a church.
II. At this meeting, discuss the purpose for organizing a new church; then codify and adopt the same into a resolution.

III. At this meeting (and subsequent meetings), there are several factors to be considered in organizing a new church. Each area is vitally important and must be given careful consideration.

   A. Structure: Methodology for a Meaningful Ministry
      1. Organization: identify church's role, set goals and objectives.
      2. Personnel and staff requirements.
      3. Corporate charter, constitution, bylaws (civil).
      4. Site and facility, insurance.
      5. IRS compliance and tax exemption.
      6. Finance: ministry plan, financing plan and spending plan.

   B. Spiritual Ministry
      1. Worship (service format)
      2. Ministry plan: organizing committee
      3. Education (all ages)
      4. Fellowship (among members)

   C. Discipleship
      1. Stewardship (of abilities and financial gifts)
      2. Lay leadership development
      3. Outreach and evangelism
      4. Social ministries
         a. Family needs
         b. Services
         c. Relationship: COGIC, community, businesses, other churches

IV. Remember that the church is the body of Christ, a living organism; and that it evangelizes and witnesses through its members, energizing people with the Holy Spirit so that they may be transformed into dynamic individuals, ministering in a changing global environment.

APPENDICES

APPENDIX 1

DOCTRINES OF THE CHURCH OF GOD IN CHRIST

THE BIBLE. WE believe that the Bible is the Word of God and contains one harmonious and sufficiently complete system of doctrine. We believe in the full inspiration of the Word of God. We hold the Word of God to be the only authority in all matters and assert that no doctrine can be true or essential if it does not find a place in this Word.

The Father. We believe in God, the Father Almighty, the Author and Creator of all things. The Old Testament reveals God in diverse manners by manifesting his nature, character, and dominion. The Gospels in the New Testament give us knowledge of God the "Father" or "my Father," showing the relationship of God to Jesus as Father or representing him as the Father in the Godhead, and Jesus himself that Son (John 15:8, 14:20). Jesus also gives God the distinction of "fatherhood" to all believers when he explains God in the light of "your Father" or "your Father in Heaven" (Matt. 11:25).

The Son. We believe that Jesus Christ is the Son of God, the second person in the Godhead of the Trinity or Triune Godhead. We believe that Jesus was and is eternal in his person and nature as the Son of God who was with God in the beginning of Creation (John 1:1). We believe that Jesus Christ was born of a virgin called Mary according to the scripture (Matt. 1:18), thus giving the rise to our fundamental belief in the Virgin Birth and to all the miraculous events surrounding this phenomenon (Matt. 1:18-25). We believe that Jesus Christ became the "suffering servant" to man; this suffering servant came seeking to redeem man from sin and to reconcile him back to God, his Father (Rom. 5:10). We believe that Jesus Christ is standing now as mediator between God and man (1 Tim. 2:5).

The Holy Ghost. We believe the Holy Ghost or Holy Spirit is the third person of the Trinity; proceeds from the Father and the Son; is of the same substance; is equal in power and glory; and is, together with the Father and the Son, to be believed in, obeyed, and worshipped. The Holy Ghost is a gift bestowed upon the believer for the purpose of equipping and empowering the believer, making him a more effective witness for service in the world. He teaches and guides one in all truth (John 16:13; Acts 1:8, 8:39).

The baptism of the Holy Ghost. We believe that the baptism of the Holy Ghost is an experience subsequent to conversion and sanctification and that tongue-speaking is the consequence of the baptism of the Holy Ghost with the manifestations of the fruit of the spirit (Gal. 5:22-23; Acts 10:46, 19:6). We believe that we are not baptized with the Holy Ghost in order to be saved, but that we are baptized with the Holy Ghost because we are saved (Acts 19:1-6, John 3:5). When one receives a baptismal Holy Ghost experience, we believe one will speak with a tongue unknown to oneself according to the sovereign will of Christ. To be filled with the spirit means to be spirit-controlled as expressed by Paul in Ephesians 5:18-19. Since the charismatic demonstrations were necessary to help the early church to be successful in implementing the command of Christ, we therefore believe that a Holy Ghost experience is mandatory for all men today.

Man. We believe that man was created holy by God, composed of body and soul. We believe that man, by nature, is sinful and unholy. Being born in sin, he needs to be born again, sanctified, and cleansed from all sins by the blood of Jesus. We believe that man is saved by confessing and forsaking his sins and believing in the Lord Jesus Christ; and that having become a child of God by being born again and adopted into the family of God, he may, and should, claim the inheritance of the sons of God, namely, the baptism of the Holy Ghost.

Sin. Sin, the Bible teaches, began in the angelic world (Ezek. 28:11-19, Isa. 14:12-20) and was transmitted into the blood of the human race through disobedience and deception motivated by unbelief (1 Tim. 2:14). Adam's sin, committed by eating the forbidden fruit from the tree of the knowledge of good and evil, carried with it a permanent pollution or depraved human nature to all his descendants. This is called original sin. *Sin* can now be defined as "a volitional transgression against God and a lack of conformity to the will of God." We therefore conclude that man, by nature, is sinful and that he has fallen from a glorious and righteous state from which he was created and has become unrighteous and unholy. Man, therefore, must be restored to his state of holiness from which he has fallen by being born again (John 3:7).

Salvation. Salvation deals with the application of the work of redemption to the sinner with his restoration to divine favor and communion with God. This redemptive operation of the Holy Ghost upon sinners is brought about by repentance toward God and faith toward our Lord Jesus Christ, which brings about conversion, faith, justification, regeneration, sanctification, and the baptism of the Holy Ghost. Repentance is the work of God that results in a change of mind in respect of man's relationship with God (Matt. 3:1-2, 4:17; Acts 20:21). Faith is a certain conviction wrought in the heart by the Holy Spirit as to the truth of the Gospel and heart's trust in the promises of God in Christ (Rom. 1:17, 3:28; Matt. 9:22; Acts 26:18). Conversion is that act of God whereby he causes the regenerated sinner, in his conscious life, to turn to him in repentance and faith (2 Kings 5:15; 2 Chron. 33:12, 13; Luke 19:8, 9; Acts 8:30). Regeneration is that act of God by which the principle of the new life is implanted in man, and the governing disposition of soul is made holy, and the first holy exercise of this new disposition is secured. Sanctification is that gracious and continuous operation of the Holy Ghost by which he delivers the justified sinner from the pollution of sin, renews his whole nature in the image of God, and enables him to perform good works (Rom. 6:4, 5:6; Col. 2:12, 13:1).

Angels. The Bible uses the term *angel* (a heavenly body) clearly and primarily to denote messengers or ambassadors of God with such scripture references as Revelation 4:5, which indicates their duty in heaven to praise God (Ps. 103:20), to do God's will (Matt. 18:10), to behold his face. But since heaven must come down to earth, they also have a mission to earth. The Bible indicates that they accompanied God in the Creation and also that they will accompany Christ in his return in glory.

Demons. Demons denote unclean or evil spirits; they are sometimes called devils or demoniac beings. They are evil spirits, belonging to the unseen or spiritual realm, embodied in human beings. The Old Testament refers to the prince of demons, sometimes called Satan (adversary) or the devil, as having power and wisdom, taking the habitation of other forms such as the serpent (Gen. 3:1). The New Testament speaks of the devil as temper (Matt. 4:3), and it goes on to tell the works of Satan, the devil, and demons as combating righteousness and good in any form, proving to be adversaries to the saint. Their chief power is exercised to destroy the mission of Jesus Christ. It can well be said that the Christian church believes in demons, Satan, and devils. We believe in their power and purpose. We believe they can be subdued and conquered, as in the commandment, to the believer by Jesus. "In my name they shall cast out Satan and the works of the devil and to resist him and then he will flee [*withdraw*] from you" (Mark 16:17).

The church. The church forms a spiritual unity of which Christ is the divine head. It is animated by one spirit, the Spirit of Christ. It professes one faith, shares our hope, and serves one King. It is the citadel of the truth and God's agency for communicating to believers all spiritual blessings. The church, then, is the object of our faith rather than of knowledge. The name of our church, Church of God in Christ, is supported by 1 Thessalonians 2:14 and other passages in the Pauline Epistles. The word *church* or "ekklesia" was first applied to the Christian society by Jesus Christ in Matthew 16:18, the occasion being that of his benediction of Peter at Caesarea Philippi.

The Second Coming of Christ. We believe in the Second Coming of Christ, that he shall come from heaven to earth personally, bodily, visibly (Acts 1:11; Titus 2:13; Matt. 16:27, 24:30, 25:30; Luke 21:27; John 1:14, 17; Titus 2:11) and that the church, the bride, will be caught up to meet him in the air (1 Thess. 4:16-17). We admonish all who have this hope to purify themselves, as he is pure.

Divine healing. The Church of God in Christ believes in and does practice divine healing. It is a commandment of Jesus to the apostles (Mark 16:18). Jesus affirms his teachings on healing by explaining to his disciples, who were to be apostles, that healing the afflicted is by faith (Luke 9:40-41). Therefore, we believe that healing by faith in God has scriptural support and ordained authority. St. James's writings in his epistles encourage elders to pray for the sick, to lay hands upon them, and to anoint them with oil, and that prayers with faith shall heal the sick and the Lord shall raise them up. Healing is still practiced widely and frequently in the Church of God in Christ, and testimonies to healings in our church testify to this fact.

Miracles. The Church of God in Christ believes that miracles occur to convince men that the Bible is God's Word. A *miracle* can be defined as "an extraordinary visible act of divine power, wrought by the efficient agency of the will of God, which has as its final cause the vindication of the righteousness of God's Word." We believe that the works of God, which were performed during the beginnings of Christianity, do and will occur even today wherein God is preached. Faith in Christ is exercised. The Holy Ghost is active, and the Gospel is promulgated in the truth (Acts 5:15, 6:8, 9:40; Luke 4:36, 7:14-15, 5:5-6; Mark 14:15).

Ordinances of the church. It is generally admitted that for an ordinance to be valid, it must have been instituted by Christ. When we speak of ordinances of the church, we are speaking of those instituted by Christ, in which by sensible signs the grace of God in Christ and the benefits of the covenant of grace to God. The Church of God in Christ then recognizes only three ordinances as having been instituted by Christ himself and therefore binding upon the church practice.

A. THE LORD'S SUPPER (HOLY COMMUNION): The Lord's Supper symbolizes the Lord's death and suffering for the benefit and in the place of his people. It also symbolizes the believer's participation in the crucified Christ. It represents not only the death of Christ as the object of faith that unites the believers to Christ but also the effect of this act as giving life, strength, and joy to the soul. The communicant, by faith, enters into a special spiritual union of his soul with the glorified Christ.

B. FEET WASHING: Feet washing is practiced and recognized as an ordinance in our church because Christ, by his example, showed that humility characterized greatness in the Kingdom of God and that service rendered to others gave evidence that humility, motivated by love, exists. These services are held subsequent to the Lord's Supper; however, its regularity is left to the discretion of the pastor in charge.

C. WATER BAPTISM: We believe that water baptism is necessary, as instructed by Christ in John 3:5, "Unless man be born again of water and of the spirit." However, we do not believe that water baptism alone is a means of salvation, but as an outward demonstration that one has already had a conversion experience and has accepted Christ as his personal Savior. As Pentecostals, we practice immersion in preference to "sprinkling" because immersion corresponds more closely to the death, burial, and resurrection of our Lord (Col. 2:12). It also symbolizes regeneration and purification more than any other mode. Therefore, we practice immersion as our mode of baptism—baptism formula. We believe that we should use the formula given us by Christ for all *baptisms*: "In the name of the Father and of the Son and of the Holy Ghost" (Matt. 28:19).

APPENDIX 2

CONTRASTS OF SOCIAL AND PASTORAL CONVERSATION

Social conversations concentrate on	Pastoral conversations concentrate on
External subjects: weather, world, events, sports	The person: unique identity
Maintaining a congenial atmosphere	Accepting tension areas
Comfort through avoiding	Comfort through facing
Sharing stories: experiences, mutual trading	Facilitating the person sharing herself/himself
Being pleasant and positive	Being understanding, empathetic
What should be	What is—as a step to what should be
Generalizing, universalizing: what they say, what people do	Being specific: what you think, feel, do
Being helpful or entertaining	Being helpful by intimate sharing
Religion: differences between churches, services, ministers	God and my/your relationship to the transcendent/imminent
People in general	Significant relationships of the person
What has happened	What is happening
Tends toward literal repeating back what was said	Utilizes paraphrases
Moves toward empathy and fusion with other	Empathetic understanding and recognition and respect for each other's boundaries

Author: Unknown

APPENDIX 3

TEN KEYS TO LEADERSHIP

"LEAD FROM YOUR HEART"

- Select great people!
- Bridge and build relationships!
- Communicate clear expectations!
- Teach and coach methods—daily!
- Challenge people to be their best!
- Be fair and consistent!
- Be approachable—allow mistakes!
- Praise first (publicly)—critique second (privately!)
- Allow people input, and make them the solution!
- Make people feel important and appreciated!

"MANAGE FROM YOUR MIND"

APPENDIX 4

FACTORS IN NONVERBAL COMMUNICATION

DRESS

Does the way you dress create the impression you want to create? How may you improve that impression?

EXPRESSIONS, GESTURES, AND BODY LANGUAGE

Are you aware of what your body and your face are communicating to others? Is what you say in line with what your body and face show?

TONE OF VOICE

Do your words say the same things as your tone of voice?

EYE CONTACT

Are you conveying through your eyes what you really want to communicate? Are you seeing other people through their eyes?

MUSCLES

Are your muscles relaxed? If not, how are they communicating tension to others?

HUMOR

How are you using your sense of humor in communicating?

EXTERNALS

What does your choice of friends, job, hobbies, automobile tell others about you?

WHAT ELSE?

APPENDIX 5

BEHAVIOR THAT CAN ENCOURAGE ACTIVE LISTENING

- Posture
- Use of space
- Respecting personal space
- Body Language
- Touch
- Looking Attentive
- Eye Contact
- Gesturing
- Nonverbal Contact Prompts
- Reflection
- Silence
- Courtesy

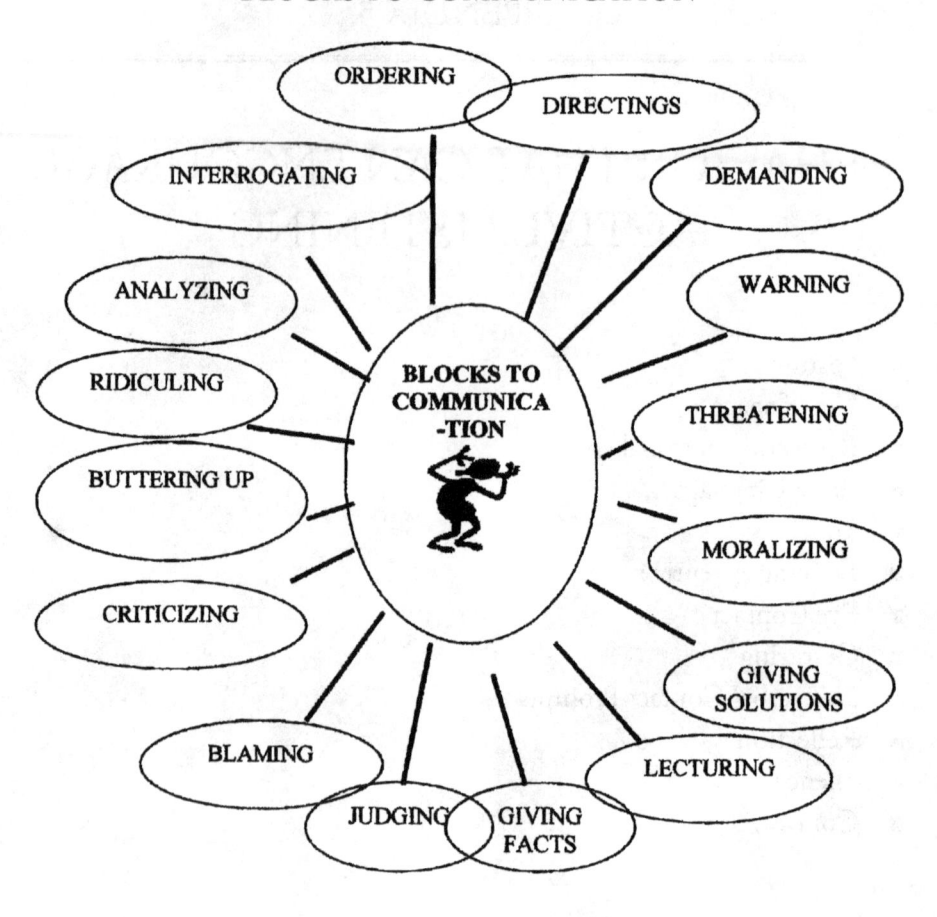

BLOCKS TO COMMUNICATION

- ORDERING
- DIRECTINGS
- DEMANDING
- WARNING
- THREATENING
- MORALIZING
- GIVING SOLUTIONS
- LECTURING
- GIVING FACTS
- JUDGING
- BLAMING
- CRITICIZING
- BUTTERING UP
- RIDICULING
- ANALYZING
- INTERROGATING

BLOCKS TO COMMUNICATION

APPENDIX 6

WHAT IS PARLIAMENTARY LAW?

PARLIAMENTARY LAW IS the code of rules and ethics for working together in groups. It provides the means for translating beliefs and ideas into effective group action. It is logic and common sense crystallized in law.

Parliamentary procedure is easy to learn. It is essentially common sense. It is simple to understand and easy to use. After a little practice, one feels at home with parliamentary procedures. It works wonders in meetings. It gives confidence and power to those who master it. It enables members and organizations to present, consider, and carry out their ideas with efficiency and harmony.

It is true that parliamentary law can be used to destroy as well as to construct. However, it can be used destructively only when a majority of the members are ignorant of their parliamentary rights.

WHAT ORGANIZATIONS MUST OBSERVE PARLIAMENTARY LAW?

All organizations, such as business, cultural, religious, social, fraternal, professional, educational, labor, civic, scientific, medical, and governmental, are subject to the principles and rules of common parliamentary law. All profit and nonprofit corporations, associations, boards, councils, commissions, and committees of government must observe its rules.

WHEN MUST ORGANIZATIONS OBSERVE PARLIAMENTARY LAW?

The court held that all groups, with the exception of state, national, and international governmental bodies, must follow general parliamentary law whenever they are meeting to transact business. If, however, a group meets solely for other purposes—for example, social or educational—it is, of course, not subject to parliamentary rules.

Even a small group—for example, a finance committee or a church board—must observe parliamentary law. However, the procedure in such groups is usually more informal than in a large convention.

When a group meets for the purpose of presenting proposals, discussing them, and arriving at decisions, parliamentary procedure is not only helpful but also indispensable. In all organizations, the rules of procedures must be observed if the actions of the assembly are to be legal. When groups are making decisions, the time-tested process of parliamentary procedures will always be necessary.

WHERE PARLIAMENTARY RULES ARE FOUND

The four basic sources of the parliamentary rules governing a particular organization, arranged in the order of their rank, are as follows:

1. Law. The law, consisting of the common law of parliamentary procedure and the status enacted by federal, state, or local governments, is the highest source of parliamentary rules for any organization.
2. Charter. The charter, granted by government to an incorporated organization, ranks second as a source. The charter, granted by a parent organization to a constituent or component unit of the organization, ranks next to its charter from government.
3. Bylaws. Any provisions of the bylaws of a parent organization that regulate the constituent or component units of the organization ranks ahead of the bylaws adopted by the units.

4. Adopted parliamentary authority. The book adopted by an organization as its authority on all procedural questions not covered by the law or its charters, bylaw, or adopted rules completes the sources of the parliamentary rules governing an organization. A parliamentary authority is a compilation of the parliamentary rules from all of these sources, assembled and organized for convenient reference.

REQUIREMENTS FOR A PARLIAMENTARY AUTHORITY

Each organization adopts, as a parliamentary authority, a code that governs the procedures of the organization in all situations not covered by rules from a higher source. Because of its importance to the organization, the parliamentary authority should be chosen with great care.

A parliamentary authority should be so clear and simple that anyone can understand it. It should be organized so that reference to the rules is quick and accurate, and it should be so complete that no other book or research will be needed. It should omit needless or outmoded procedures but must include all current, practical, businesslike procedures. It must present parliamentary law so accurately that the courts will uphold any action taken according to the rules it states. If the rules of the adopted parliamentary authority do not conform to the law, the organization that follows it may find itself in legal difficulties.

FUNDAMENTAL PRINCIPLES OF PARLIAMENTARY LAW

The most important principles of parliamentary procedure are the following:

1. The purpose of parliamentary procedure is to facilitate the transaction of business and to promote cooperation and harmony.
2. All members have equal rights, privileges, and obligations.
3. The majority vote decides.
4. The rights of the minority must be protected.

5. Full and free discussion of every proposition presented for decision is an established right of members.
6. Every member has the right to know the meaning of the question before the assembly and what its effect will be.
7. All meetings must be characterized by fairness and by good faith.

CLASSIFICATION OF MOTIONS

A. Classes of Motions

Motions are classified, according to their purposes and characteristics, into four groups:

- Main motions
- Subsidiary motions
- Privileged motions
- Incidental motions

   1. Main Motions
   Main motions are the most important and most frequently used. The main motion is the foundation of the conduct of business. Its purpose is to bring substantive proposals before the assembly for consideration and action. After it is stated by the presiding officer, the main motion becomes the subject for deliberation and decision.

   There are three main motions that have specific names:

   - Reconsider
   - Rescind
   - Resume consideration

2. Subsidiary Motions

   Subsidiary motions are alternative aids for changing, considering, and disposing of the main motion. Consequently, they are subsidiary to it. Subsidiary motions are usually applied to the main motion, but some of them may be applied to certain other motions.

   The most frequently used subsidiary motions are as follows:

   - Postpone temporarily (lay on the table)
   - Vote immediately (previous question)
   - Limit debate
   - Postpone definitely
   - Refer to a committee
   - Amend
   - Postpone indefinitely

3. Privileged Motions

   Privileged motions have no direct connections with the main motion before the assembly. They are emergency motions of such urgency that they are entitled immediate consideration. They relate to the members and to the organization rather than to particular items of business. Privileged motions would be main motions but for their urgency. Because of their urgency, they are given the privilege of being considered ahead of other motions that are before the assembly.

   The privileged motions are the following:

   - Adjourn
   - Recess
   - Question of privilege

4. Incidental Motions

   Incidental motions arise only incidentally out of the business before the assembly. They do not relate directly to the main motion but usually relate to matters that are incidental to the conduct of the meeting. Incidental motions may be offered at any time when they are needed. They have no order of precedence, and it is only necessary that they be disposed of as soon as they arise and prior to the business out of which they arise.

   Appeal, suspend rules, and object to considerations are motions and are therefore decided by vote of the assembly. Point of order, parliamentary inquiry, withdrawing a motion, division of a question, and division of the assembly technically are classified as motions. Actually, they are requests directed to the presiding officer and decided by him. Two of these requests—withdraw a motion and division of questions—if not granted by the presiding officer, may be presented as motions for decision by vote of the assembly. The most frequently used incidental motions are as follows:

   - Appeal
   - Suspend rules
   - Object of consideration
   - Point of order
   - Parliamentary inquiry
   - Withdraw a motion
   - Division of a question
   - Division of the assembly

THE CHIEF PURPOSES OF MOTIONS

PURPOSE	MOTION
Present an idea for consideration and action	Main motion Resolution Consider subject informally
Improve a pending motion	Amend Division of question
Regulate or cut off debate	Limit or extended debate Vote immediately
Delay a decision	Refer to committee Postpone definitely Postpone temporarily Recess
Suppress a proposal	Object to consideration Postpone indefinitely Withdraw a motion
Meet an emergency	Question of privilege Suspend rules
Gain information on a pending motion	Parliamentary inquiry Request for information Request to as member a question Question of privilege
Question the decision of the presiding officer	Point of order Appeal from decision of chair
Enforce rights and privileges	Division of assembly Division of question Parliamentary inquiry Point of order Appeal from decision of chair
Consider a question again	Resume consideration Reconsider Rescind Renew a motion
Change an action already taken	Reconsider Rescind Amend by new motion
Terminate a meeting	Adjourn Recess

Order of Precedence	Can Interrupt?	Requires Second?	Debatable	Amendable	Vote Required?	Applies to what other motions?	Can have what other motions applied to it? (In addition to withdraw?)
Privileged motions							
1. Adjourn	NO	YES	NO	NO	MAJORITY	NONE	NONE
2. Recess	NO	YES	YES*	YES*	MAJORITY	NONE	AMEND*
3. Question of privilege	YES	NO	NO	NO	NONE	NONE	NONE
Subsidiary motions							
4. Postpone temporarily	NO	YES	NO	NO	MAJORITY	MAIN MOTION (debatable)	NONE
5. Vote immediately	NO	YES	NO	NO	2/3	MOTION	NONE
6. Limit debate	NO	YES	YES*	YES*	2/3	DEBATABLE MOTION	AMEND*
7. Postpone definitely	NO	YES	YES*	YES*	MAJORITY	MAIN MOTION	AMEND* VOTE IMM., LIMIT DEBATE
8. Refer to committee	NO	YES	YES*	YES*	MAJORITY	MAIN MOTION	AMEND* VOTE IMM., LIMIT DEBATE
9. Amend	NO	YES	YES	YES	MAJORITY	REWORDABLE MOTIONS	VOTE IMM., LIMIT DEBATE
10. Postpone indefinitely	NO	YES	YES	NO	MAJORITY	MAIN MOTION	LIMIT DEBATE
Main motions							
11. A. The main motion	NO	YES	YES	YES	MAJORITY	NONE	SPECIFIC MAIN, SUBSID., OBJ. TO CONS.
11. B. Specific main motions							

	Can interrupt?	Requires second?	Debatable	Amendable	Vote required?	Applies to what other motions?	Can have what other motions applied to it (in addition to withdraw)?
Reconsider	YES	YES	YES	YES	MAJORITY	MAIN MOTION	VOTE IMM., LIMIT DEBATE
Rescind	NO	YES	NO	NO	MAJORITY	MAIN MOTION	VOTE IMM., LIMIT DEBATE
Resume consideration	NO	YES	NO	NO	MAJORITY	MAIN MOTION	NONE
No order of precedence							
Incidental Motions							
A. Motions							
Appeal	YES	YES	YES	NO	MAJORITY	DECISION OF CHAIR	VOTE IMM., LIMIT DEBATE
Suspend rules	NO	YES	NO	NO	2/3	NONE	NONE
Object to consideration	YES	YES	NO	NO	2/3 neg.	MAIN MOTION	NONE
B. Request							
Point of order	YES	NO	NO	NO	NONE	ANY ERROR	NONE
Parliamentary inquiry	YES	NO	NO	NO	NONE	NONE	NONE
Withdraw a motion	YES	NO	NO	NO	NONE	ALL MOTIONS	NONE
Division of questions	NO	NO	NO	NO	NONE	MAIN MOTION INDECISVE	NONE
Division of assembly	YES	NO	NO	NO	NONE	VOTE	NONE

* Restricted

APPENDIX 7

WRITING AND IMPLEMENTING THE VISION

THIS CLINIC WILL concern itself with three biblical principles and their relationship to "visioneering." Our overall theme is "Visions: Turning Impossibilities into the Possible," with a divine strategy to turn the possible into reality!

The three biblical principles are as follows:

I. COMMUNICATING THE VISION, MISSION, PURPOSE, AND A STRATEGIC MINISTRY PLAN.

> "And the Lord answered me, and said, write the vision, and make it plain upon tables, that he may runt that readeth it" (Hab. 2:2).

You must communicate the vision clearly and develop a strategy that transfers vision clearly and transfers vision ownership to the people, thereby activating renewal, enthusiasm, and momentum.

Ministry plan (*revealing your mission*). The vision for your ministry originated in the mind of God. He called and commissioned you to communicate it clearly to others so that they can implement it through to completion. Set up "visioneering" sessions with the congregation.

These visioneering sessions are where you will pray and share God's vision for the ministry with the ministry, with membership. It is here that you must clearly and articulately write down what God has given you. Next, develop and activate a long-range strategic ministry plan that transfers the vision into the hearts of the people. God (and the people) is relying on effective leadership to see the vision come to pass.

In order to make better, informed leadership decisions, you must have a ministry checkup (removing vision barriers). Once the vision has been developed and clearly articulated, barriers must be removed.

Analysis of church vital systems must include

- existing vision and current ministry strategy;
- finances (capability for a building project);
- administration and staffing for the vision;
- surveys of leadership, congregation, community, and church visitors;
- growth trends, potential, and barriers; and
- site and facilities (existing and proposed).

II. DESIGNING CUSTOMIZED VISION-DRIVE FACILITIES

> "And he gave some, apostles; and some, prophets; and some, evangelists; and some, pastors and teachers; for the perfecting of the saints, for the work of the ministry, for the edifying of the body of Christ" (Eph. 4:11-12).

Vision Plan (Vision Bearers Released)

The vision plan must be a customized, lay ministry-based project management process according to Ephesians 4:12's principles to integrate the people's gifts and talents into the fulfillment of the church vision, while protecting the ministries that are so important to continued church health.

The results are increased involvement, enthusiasm, momentum, and congregational ownership of the vision. Assign service work to members and others so as to avoid "pastoral burnout."

III. CAMPAIGNING (VISION GOALS REALIZED)

> "For which of you, intending to build a tower, sitteth not down first, and counteth the cost, whether he have sufficient to finish it?" (Luke 14:28).

Tell the membership to ask the Lord, "What do you want me to do for you and for the vision you have shared with our pastor—to see it come to pass?"

- Count up the costs, both ministerial and financial of the vision (project).
- Complete the due diligence, which will save you time and money, ensuring success.

Results will be

1. increased spiritual maturity,
2. more fellowship in the community,
3. increased financial giving, and
4. multiple ministry involvement and participation.

HANDOUTS

HANDOUT NO. 1

Superintendent's Job Overview

THE DISTRICT SUPERINTENDENT shall, in every way, assist the bishop in developing the spiritual and financial life of the jurisdiction. His duties are the following:

A. To travel through his district so that he may oversee the spiritual and temporal affairs of the churches at least twice a year and to give the local pastor in his district his personal influence and assistance when it is needed.

B. To have charge of all the evangelists and local pastors in his district in the absence of the bishop or his assistant.

C. To inform the churches in his district their duties to the local church and district, state, and national church.

D. To counsel with pastors in his district regarding their pastoral responsibilities when needed.

E. To preside in the annual district meeting. He is to encourage the members in the district meeting to support their local churches with their faithful attendance and to finance and maintain a working and effective fellowship among the pastors.

F. To assist the bishop in collecting the finances for the district, jurisdictional, and national work as directed by the bishop.

G. To mediate disputes involving the pastor and members upon request of the pastor. If arbitration is needed, the superintendent shall then commission an investigating committee to hear the dispute or grievance. The district superintendent shall be one of the members of this committee unless there is a conflict of interest. The findings shall be reported to the office of the bishop in writing for disposition.

H. To take charge, when approved by the bishop, of a local church within his district if the pastor dies, resigns, becomes incapacitated, or is removed, until another pastor can be appointed by the bishop.
I. To see that (where state or national monies have been used to build or buy a church) all charters, deeds, and other conveyances of church property in his district conform to the discipline and laws of the church, county, state, or country within which such property is situated.
J. To promote all the interest of the churches within his district with the cooperation of the pastors.

HANDOUT NO. 2

First Jurisdiction—Illinois Executive Leadership Institute

- MISSION STATEMENT (Jurisdiction)

    We—the First Jurisdiction—Illinois Church of God in Christ, in conjunction with the national church—are committed to work under the power, direction, and authority of God to fulfill the Great Commission (Matt. 28:19-20, Mark 16:15-18) by providing a healing, caring, and evangelistic ministry for our member churches.

    With a global perspective, our religious, moral, and theological responsibility requires us to identify, develop, and realize various church development programs. The focus will be on planning, organizing, physical, spiritual, educational, and economic delivery systems.

    Implementation of the said programs will be carried out through our present departments and auxiliaries.

- MISSION STATEMENT (Leadership Institute)

    The Pastoral Executive Leadership Institute is committed to providing an opportunity for the development of pastors and others into effective informed and well-trained leaders.

    Through the institute, both ecclesiastical and civil dimensions will be equally important, assisting the pastors in classes, customized seminars, workshops, and dissemination of economic information.

HANDOUT NO. 3

FIRST JURISDICTION—ILLINOIS

CHURCH OF GOD IN CHRIST

COMMITTEE ON THE CONSTITUTION

Ocie Booker, chairman and superintendent

Pastor Isaiah Grover, vice chairman

Mother Eleanor Harrington, secretary

Sister Jane Crossley

Mother Charolette Eades

Douglas Moye, superintendent

Superintendent Thomas Jackson

Superintendent Robert East

FIRST JURISDICTION—ILLINOIS CHURCH OF GOD IN CHRIST MISSION STATEMENT

We—the First Jurisdiction—Illinois Church of God in Christ, in conjunction with the national church—are committed to work under the power, direction, and authority of God to fulfill the Great Commission (Matt. 28:19, 20; Mark 16:15, 18) by providing a healing, caring, and evangelistic ministry for our member churches.

With a global perspective, our religious, moral, and theological responsibility requires us to identify, develop, and realize various church development programs. The focus will be on planning and organizing physical, spiritual, educational, and economic delivery systems. Implementation of said programs will be carried out through our present departments and auxiliaries.

THE CONSTITUTION OF FIRST JURISDICTION—ILLINOIS CHURCH OF GOD IN CHRIST DECLARATION OF FAITH AND PREAMBLE

We, the members of the First Jurisdiction—Illinois Church of God in Christ, hold the Holy Scripture as contained in the Old and New Testaments of our Bible as our rule of faith and practice.

We believe that governments are God-given institutions for the benefit of mankind. We admonish and exhort our members to honor magistrates and civil authorities and to respect and obey civil laws.

We dedicate this charter to the memory and honor of the late Mother Lillian Brooks Coffey, who became a great leader of Christian women as the general supervisor of the Women's Department in the Church of God in Christ worldwide; and the late Mother Mary Davis, a woman of great faith and love for God's people; and other pioneering men and women who initiated the mission of the Church of God in Christ in the state of Illinois.

Our most profound respect goes to the late Bishop William Matthew Roberts (1953), who provided the courageous, fearless, and faithful leadership in the planting of the Church of God in Christ throughout the states of Illinois, Indiana, and Wisconsin.

And to our greatly missed and most revered prelate of First Jurisdiction—Illinois Church of God in Christ, the late Bishop Louis Henry Ford (1995), who started his gospel ministry on the street corners of Chicago, Illinois, and ascended to the headship of the church as the presiding bishop of the Church of God in Christ Inc.

The lifework of these great men and women of faith is responsible for much of our progress today in the Church of God in Christ.

Wherefore, God is not ashamed to be called their God.

JURISDICTIONAL CONSTITUTION

RESOLUTION

WHEREAS, article 3, section C, paragraph 3 in jurisdictional assemblies of the Constitution of the Church of God in Christ Inc. provides that "jurisdictional assemblies shall be presided over by their respective bishops." Jurisdictional assemblies shall have the right to adopt such laws and rules for their government as may be deemed necessary and proper, but shall not adopt any law, rule, or regulation in conflict with or repugnant to the charter, constitution, laws, rules and regulations of the general church; and

WHEREAS, First Jurisdiction—Illinois desires to be patterned after the National General Assembly to comply with the constitutional provisions in the election of delegates to the general assembly; and

WHEREAS, First Jurisdiction—Illinois works in partnership with the national church providing leadership and oversight of the life and mission of the Church of God in Christ in said jurisdiction; and

WHEREAS, inasmuch as First Jurisdiction—Illinois has the power and authority to adopt such provisions for its self-governance;

NOW THEREFORE IT BE RESOLVED THAT:

In order for First Jurisdiction—Illinois to more fully carry out its duties and responsibilities, the jurisdiction hereby adopts the following rules of procedure for the governing and operation of the jurisdiction.

Adopted this_____ day of_____1996 by the First Jurisdiction—Illinois, Assembly, Church of God in Christ.

_____
Chairman
Jurisdictional Assembly

_____
Secretary
Jurisdictional Assembly

ARTICLE I. STRUCTURE: CIVIL AND ECCLESIASTICAL

PART I. CIVIL STRUCTURE—FIRST JURISDICTION—ILLINOIS CHURCH OF GOD IN CHRIST

A. The civil officers of First Jurisdiction—Illinois shall be president, first vice president, secretary, treasurer, assistant treasurer, and such other officers as the corporation shall establish.
   1. The *president* shall preside at all meetings and shall have general supervision of the business affairs of the corporation and shall make an annual report of the status and condition of the corporation to the board of directors. The president shall sign all certificates, contracts, deeds, and other instruments of the corporation. During the absence or the disability of the president, the *first vice president* shall exercise all the powers and discharge all the duties of the president.
   2. The *secretary* shall keep minutes of all meetings, shall have charge of the seal and corporate books, shall make such reports and perform such other duties as is required of him by the corporation, and shall sign all certificates, contracts, deeds, etc.
   3. The *treasurer* shall have custody of all monies and securities of the corporation and shall keep regular books of account. He shall disburse the funds of the corporation in payment of just demands against the corporation or as may be ordered by the corporation. From time to time, as may be required of him, he shall make an accounting of all his transactions as treasurer and of the financial condition.
   4. The *assistant treasurer* shall perform duties of the treasurer in his absence, disability, or as directed by the corporation.
   5. *Tenure of office.* The officers of the corporation shall hold office during good behavior or until their successors are elected and qualified.

PART II. ECCLESIASTICAL STRUCTURE—FIRST JURISDICTION—ILLINOIS CHURCH OF GOD IN CHRIST

A. JURISDICTIONAL BISHOP

The bishop of First Jurisdiction—Illinois shall be appointed or removed by the presiding bishop with the approval of the General Board of the Church of God in Christ Inc., and he shall have the following qualifications, powers, and duties:

1. Qualifications
   a. He must be an ordained elder in the Church of God in Christ who is in good standing.
   b. He must have at least ten (10) years' experience in the pastoral ministry.
   c. He must meet the biblical qualifications of a bishop according to 1 Timothy 3:1-7.
   d. He must have the necessary skills to plan and implement programs for spiritual growth and development of those who serve under his administration in First Jurisdiction—Illinois.

2. Duties and Responsibilities
   a. He shall be the chief executive officer of the First Ecclesiastical Jurisdiction, Illinois, Church of God in Christ.
   b. He shall have authority to appoint and/or remove district superintendents, heads of all departments, and all other state officers in his ecclesiastical jurisdiction unless otherwise provided for by the constitution of the Church of God in Christ Inc.
   c. The bishop of First Jurisdiction—Illinois shall have the authority to appoint and ordain elders with his jurisdiction.

3. The bishop of First Jurisdiction—Illinois shall be the representative of the Church of God in Christ with respect to all church matters in this ecclesiastical jurisdiction and shall have general supervision

over all departments and churches in First Jurisdiction—Illinois Church of God in Christ.
4. The bishop of First Jurisdiction—Illinois shall be responsible for planning and implementing the program for the jurisdiction's annual spring conference (workers' meeting) and the annual holy convocation.
5. The bishop of First Jurisdiction—Illinois is responsible for upholding the provisions of the constitution and the provisions of the general assembly in his jurisdiction. He shall serve as a liaison between the national church and First Jurisdiction—Illinois Church of God in Christ.

B. DISTRICTS

Within each ecclesiastical jurisdiction, there is a smaller unit of churches called districts. The districts are presided over by a superintendent. The purpose of the districts in First Jurisdiction—Illinois are as follows:

1. Provide for the pastoral care of local congregations within the district.
2. Provide leadership recruitment, preparation, and support according to the policies and standards of the Church of God in Christ and First Jurisdiction—Illinois.
3. Foster the development of the departments and auxiliaries in First Jurisdiction—Illinois.
4. Plan for the growth and outreach of missions in First Jurisdiction—Illinois.
5. Be willing to participate and pledge their support in the programs of First Jurisdiction—Illinois.
6. Administer the affairs of First Jurisdiction—Illinois, Church of God in Christ in each respective area.
7. Discharge all jurisdictional and national financial responsibilities and obligations.

C. DISTRICT ASSEMBLIES

In compliance with the constitutional provisions in the election of delegates to the jurisdictional assembly and the general assembly of the Church of

God in Christ, there shall be a district assembly in each district of First Jurisdiction—Illinois. The district assemblies shall be patterned after the assembly of First Jurisdiction—Illinois and/or the general assembly of the Church of God in Christ Inc. The district assembly is presided over by the district superintendent.

The membership of the district assembly shall be

1. district superintendent,
2. district missionary,
3. pastors of local churches,
4. ordained elders,
5. district department heads,
6. licensed missionaries,
7. one lay delegate from each local church, and
8. widows of founders of local churches.

D. DISTRICT SUPERINTENDENTS

As stated hereinabove, the jurisdictional bishop has the authority to choose and appoint district superintendents.

1. Duties
   a. To travel through his districts so that he may oversee the spiritual and the temporal affairs of the churches at least twice a year, and to give the local pastor in his district his personal influence and assistance when there is a need.
   b. To have charge of all the evangelists and local pastors in his district in the absence of the bishop and/or his assistant.
   c. To inform the churches in his district of their duties to the local church and district, state, and national church.
   d. To counsel with pastors in his district regarding their pastoral responsibilities when needed.
   e. To preside in the annual district meeting. He is to encourage the members in the district meeting to support their local churches

with their faithful attendance and finance and to maintain a working and effective fellowship among the pastors.
f. To assist the bishop in collecting the finances for the district, jurisdictional, and national work as directed by the bishop.
g. To mediate disputes involving the pastor and members upon request of the pastor. If arbitration is needed, the superintendent shall then commission an investigating committee to hear the dispute or grievance. The district superintendent shall be one of the members of this committee unless there is a conflict of interest. The findings shall be reported to the office of the bishop in writing for disposition.
h. To take charge of a local church within his district if the pastor dies, resigns, becomes incapacitated, or is removed, until another pastor can be appointed by the bishop.
i. To see to it that (where state or national monies have been used to build or buy a church) all charters, deeds, and other conveyances of church property in his district conform to the discipline and laws of the church, county, state, or country within which such property is situated.
j. To promote all the interest of the church within his district with the cooperation of the pastors.

E. Departments

1. Women's Department

There shall be a Women's Department in the general church and in each ecclesiastical jurisdiction.

A. Jurisdictional Supervisors

The national supervisor shall have the power to appoint and remove a jurisdictional supervisor, who shall supervise the work of the Women's Department in the jurisdiction of her appointment. No such appointment or removal shall be made unless the same is consented to and approved by the bishop presiding in the jurisdiction and by the presiding bishop of the general church. The jurisdictional supervisor shall be empowered to issue license in the jurisdiction to all eligible women for state and district recognition and as otherwise authorized by the general supervisor of women in the Church of God in Christ Inc. Jurisdictional supervisors shall have the power to appoint and remove district missionaries in the jurisdictions of their appointment. No such appointment or removal shall be made unless the same is consented to by both district superintendent and the bishop presiding in that jurisdiction. The Women's Department shall supervise the following:

1. Prayer and Bible band
2. Young Women's Christian Council
3. Purity class
4. Sunshine band
5. Any other auxiliary, national, state, or local that the national supervisor and/or general board shall deem necessary for the women's work

The jurisdictional supervisor shall have the authority to appoint or remove jurisdictional officers from such auxiliaries subject to the approval of the jurisdictional bishop.

The appointment and removal of local officers of such auxiliaries shall be exercised by the local pastor.

B. District Missionaries

District missionaries are chosen and appointed by the state supervisor, subject to the approval of the jurisdictional bishop, the district superintendent, and her pastor. The duties of a district missionary are the following:

1. To act under the supervision of the jurisdictional supervisor and district superintendent.

2. To assist the pastor upon his request in organizing auxiliaries and bands within the local church.
3. To teach women in the churches to be subject and loyal to their pastors, bishops, and supervisors.
4. To inform and remind the churches in her district at least two times a year of their responsibilities toward the local church and district, state, and national work.
5. To assist the district superintendent in collecting the finances for the district, jurisdictional, and national work.
6. To review the work of each missionary in the district meetings. At such times, an offering of appreciation shall be given for her labor and service.
7. To implement the programs and orders of the state supervisor. To promote all the interest of the church within the district with the cooperation of the district superintendent and pastors.

C. Missionaries

The duties of a missionary are

1. to evangelize the work of the churches as much as lies within her power;
2. to travel and conduct revival meetings;
3. to carry a gospel of comfort and deliverance to hospitals, jails, convalescent homes, and the like; and
4. to visit the shut-ins and give physical assistance when there is a need.

All missionaries are subject to their pastors and must-be supporters of their local church before venturing into the gospel field.

Licensing of Missionaries

1. Missionaries must meet qualifications as set by the church; however, it is a pastor's prerogative to request and receive evangelist license for a missionary of his congregation that he feels is qualified in all aspects.

2. No missionary shall be licensed without being recommended by her pastor. All such licenses are issued by the jurisdictional supervisor of the Women's Department.

2. The Sunday School Department

   There shall be a Sunday School Department for training and enlightening children and adults in the scriptural understanding and doctrines of the Church of God in Christ.

   a. The Sunday School Department shall be under the supervision and direction of a jurisdictional superintendent appointed by the jurisdictional bishop.
   b. The jurisdictional bishop shall have the power to appoint or remove a jurisdictional superintendent of the Sunday School Department, who shall supervise the work of the Sunday school in the jurisdiction of his appointment.
   c. The jurisdictional superintendent of the Sunday School Department shall organize and set up the Sunday School Department at the jurisdictional level by establishing Sunday school districts therein and shall supervise the Sunday school on the state and district levels.
   d. Local churches shall have local superintendents of the Sunday schools, who shall be appointed by their respective pastors. The removal of a local superintendent shall be done by the procedure as that of any other local officer or member of the local church.

3. The Young People's Department

   There shall be a Young People's Department that shall be called the Young People's Willing Workers.

   a. The jurisdictional bishop shall have the power to appoint and remove a state president of the Young People's Department.
   b. The Young People's Department shall be under the supervision and direction of a jurisdictional president.

c. The jurisdictional president of the Young People's Department shall organize and set up the Young People's Department at the jurisdictional level and shall supervise the work of the Young People's Willing Workers in the jurisdiction of his appointment.
   d. Local churches shall have local presidents of the Young People's Department, who shall be appointed by the respective pastors. The removal of a local president shall be the same as that of any other local officer or member of the local church.

4. Department of Home and Foreign Missions

   There shall be a jurisdictional department of home and foreign missions for the spiritual and doctrinal development of missions in underdeveloped areas in both local and foreign territories.

   a. There shall be a jurisdictional president, executive secretary, treasurer, and board of directors in the said department.
   b. The jurisdictional bishop shall have the power to appoint or remove the jurisdictional president and officers of the Home and Foreign Missions in the jurisdiction of his appointment.
   c. Local churches should have a Home and Foreign Missions Department whose officers shall be appointed and removed by the pastor.

5. Department of Evangelism

   There shall be a jurisdictional department of evangelism to carry on the evangelical work and program of the church.

   a. There shall be a jurisdictional president, executive secretary, treasurer, and board of directors in the said department.
   b. The jurisdictional bishop shall appoint the officers of said department and shall have the right to remove any officer thereof.

ARTICLE II. JURISDICTIONAL ASSEMBLY

The purpose of the jurisdictional assembly in First Jurisdiction—Illinois Church of God in Christ is to make such rules and regulations over all departments of the jurisdiction and also to adopt the rules of order governing its organization, procedures, committees, and other matters as may be deemed necessary and proper for the conduct of its business. However, the jurisdictional assembly of First Jurisdiction—Illinois shall not adopt any law, rule, or regulation in conflict with or repugnant to the charter, constitution, laws, rules, and regulations of the Church of God in Christ Inc.

A. MEMBERSHIP

The membership of the assembly of First Jurisdiction—Illinois Church of God in Christ shall be

>jurisdictional bishop,
>supervisor of Women's Department,
>district superintendents,
>all pastors of local churches,
>ordained elders,
>district missionaries,
>jurisdictional department heads,
>one lay delegate elected from each jurisdictional district, and
>widows of founders of local churches.

1. No person shall be elected as an officer of this jurisdictional assembly who is not in *Persons of good standing* and fellowship with the Church of God in Christ. (Persons of good standing: those who have declared their faith in Jesus Christ as their Savior, their belief in the doctrine of the Church of God in Christ, and their willingness to submit and abide by the government of the Church of God in Christ.)

2. First Jurisdiction—Illinois assembly shall elect from its membership delegates to the general assembly.

B. OFFICERS OF THE JURISDICTIONAL ASSEMBLY

1. The permanent chairman of First Jurisdiction—Illinois assembly shall be the jurisdictional bishop, and he shall hold office as chairman of the assembly until its final adjournment. However, the permanent chairman shall have the right to appoint a presiding officer in his stead, in the event he needed to be excused or temporarily relieved from office.
2. The following officers shall be elected by the jurisdictional assembly:
   a. The secretary, who shall perform such duties as may be assigned to them by the jurisdictional assembly
   b. The parliamentarian, who shall advise the chairman as to points of the parliamentary procedure
3. The following officers shall be appointed by the chairman of the jurisdictional assembly of First Jurisdiction—Illinois.
   a. Chaplain, who shall conduct devotional services
   b. Sergeant at arms, who shall keep and maintain order in all sessions of the jurisdictional assembly

C. ELECTION AND CERTIFICATION OF DELEGATES

1. Delegates to the jurisdictional assembly—except jurisdictional bishop, supervisor of women, district superintendents, and district missionaries—shall be certified by the secretaries of their respective districts. The secretary of each jurisdictional district shall send to the jurisdictional secretary a list of such certified delegates, which list shall be registered by the jurisdictional secretary, who shall then issue to the delegates certificates of registration.
2. Delegates qualifying as bishop, supervisor of women, district superintendents, and district missionaries shall be issued certificates

of registration by the jurisdictional secretary after he has verified their respective offices.
3. Delegates to the jurisdictional assembly shall serve only for the session and time for which they were elected or for only such time that they shall hold an office that qualifies them to serve as delegates to the jurisdictional assembly.
4. If a delegate who has been elected by his jurisdictional district or has qualified as bishop, supervisor of women, district superintendent, or district missionary is refused a certificate of registration by the jurisdictional secretary, the delegate may appeal to the committee on credentials through the chairman or any officer thereof. Upon the filing of such an appeal, the chairman of the credentials committee shall forthwith convene a meeting of the credentials committee, which shall then act upon the delegate's claim. An adverse decision by the credentials committee may be appealed to the jurisdictional assembly, which is then in session, by filing an appeal with the presiding officer or assistant presiding officer of the jurisdictional assembly thereof. Upon filing of such an appeal, the presiding officer of the jurisdictional assembly shall convene a meeting of the jurisdictional assembly, which shall determine the issues presented by the delegate's appeal. The decision, by majority vote of the members of the jurisdictional assembly present and voting, shall be final and binding on all parties.
5. The secretary of the credentials committee shall keep a record of its proceedings and file certified copies thereof with the chairman of the jurisdictional assembly and the secretary of the jurisdictional assembly.

D. MEETINGS OF THE JURISDICTIONAL ASSEMBLY

The jurisdictional assembly shall meet semiannually during the state Spring Worker's Meeting and the state Holy Convocation.

A special session of the jurisdictional assembly shall be called by the jurisdictional bishop and/or the board of superintendents, giving notice thereof to all members of the jurisdiction qualified to be delegates to the jurisdictional assembly hereinabove, stating the purpose of such special session. A special session of the jurisdictional assembly shall be convened for only the purpose, or purposes, set forth in the notice calling a special session.

However, if the jurisdictional assembly is in session and has acted on any constitutional amendment requiring a vacancy to be filled, the jurisdictional assembly, then in session, is authorized to fill such vacancy or vacancies, without calling a special session thereof.

E. RULES AND REGULATIONS
   1. The jurisdictional assembly shall adopt such rules of procedure and regulations governing the conduct of its business and its organization as it may deem necessary, proper, or expedient.
   2. The jurisdictional bishop, as the ecclesiastical head and chief executive officer of the jurisdiction, is mandated to uphold the provisions of the constitution of the Church of God in Christ Inc. and serve as liaison between the national church and the jurisdiction in which he serves. Therefore, nothing in the constitution of First Jurisdiction—Illinois Church of God in Christ shall operate to deprive the bishop of First Jurisdiction—Illinois the power and authority vested in him by the Church of God in Christ Inc. or inhibit in any way the carrying out of duties delegated to his charge.

F. POWERS AND RESTRICTIONS OF THE JURISDICTIONAL ASSEMBLY

The power and authority of the jurisdictional assembly to legislate for the jurisdiction, to make rules and regulations over all departments as it may deem best are limited to the following restrictions:

1. It shall not set aside or change any of the articles of faith, nor shall it establish any new doctrines contrary to the doctrines that now exist in the Church of God in Christ and First Jurisdiction—Illinois.

2. The jurisdictional assembly shall not abolish our representative form of government or the general superintendency nor deprive it of any of the authority given it by this constitution.

No person shall be seated in the jurisdictional assembly who has not been duly elected as a delegate or an alternate by a recognized district of First Jurisdiction—Illinois Church of God in Christ.

3. The jurisdictional assembly shall not deprive the ministers or members of First Jurisdiction—Illinois Church of God in Christ of a fair trial or an appeal in case of conviction.

ARTICLE III. PASTORS' AND ELDERS' COUNCIL

The council of pastors and elders of First Jurisdiction—Illinois shall consist of all pastors and elders who are in good standing, as defined hereinabove, and shall be organized and have the following duties, to wit:

A. The officers shall be as follows:
   1. Chairman, vice chairman, secretary, treasurer, and such other officers as it may deem necessary and proper, according to the provisions in this constitution.
   2. The officers shall be elected by the majority of the council members present and voting.

B. It shall consider matters that are referred to it by the jurisdictional bishop and jurisdictional assembly and shall make a report of its findings to appropriate organs of the church.

C. It shall serve as an ecclesiastical council to try, hear, and determine cases and all other matters referred to it under the constitution or laws of the Church of God in Christ and First Jurisdiction—Illinois.

D. It shall establish such rules and regulations as it may deem necessary and proper for the conduct of its business not inconsistent with the constitution or laws of the Church of God in Christ and First Jurisdiction—Illinois.

E. It shall exercise all other powers and duties vested in it by the charter, constitution, and bylaws of the Church of God in Christ and First Jurisdiction—Illinois.

ARTICLE IV. PASTORS OF LOCAL CHURCHES

A. The pastor is the chief executive officer of the local church and shall have the general oversight and supervision thereof.
B. The pastor shall have the right to appoint and remove officers of the local church and to administer his office in accordance with the charter, constitution, and bylaws of the Church of God in Christ.
C. The pastor shall be responsible for the spiritual and doctrinal guidance of the local church.

ARTICLE V. LOCAL CHURCHES

A. The local church is the basic unit of the structural organization of the Church of God in Christ. Its membership shall consist all who have been set in order as a church by those authorized to do so after having first declared their faith in Jesus Christ as their Savior and declared their faith and belief in the doctrine of the Church of God in Christ and their willingness to submit to and abide by the government of the Church of God in Christ. The pastor of a local church shall be appointed by the jurisdictional bishop of the ecclesiastical jurisdiction of the church.
B. A local church may be established or set in order by the jurisdictional bishop or his designee.
C. No local church shall have full status in the Church of God in Christ until it has been registered by its jurisdictional bishop in the office of the general secretary, who shall then issue to the jurisdictional bishop a certificate of membership for the local church.
D. Neither a local church, whose jurisdictional bishop has not received a certificate of membership from the general secretary of the Church, nor any member thereof shall be entitled to enjoy the rights and privileges of membership in the Church of God in Christ.

E. A local church that has been accepted by the Church of God in Christ and been issued a certificate of membership shall not have the right or privilege to withdraw or sever its relations with the general church, except by and with the permission of the general jurisdictional assembly.

F. A local church may establish its own constitution and bylaws, provided the same shall not be in conflict with or repugnant to the charter, constitution, laws, and doctrine of the Church of God in Christ.

G. A local church in good standing and fellowship with the Church of God in Christ whose certificate of membership has not been suspended or revoked shall have the right to elect delegates to its jurisdictional assembly.

H. All trustees of local churches shall be members of the Church of God in Christ. In all cases where the law requires a special mode of election of church trustees, that mode must be followed. Trustees of unincorporated local churches and their successors in office shall hold title to all real and personal property for the use and benefit of the members of the church. Where, however, the law requires no particular mode of election of trustees, they all be elected by majority of the members of the congregation, present and voting, in a regular or special business meeting of the church. All special meetings of the church shall be announced on a Sunday preceding the date of the meeting and shall state the purpose of the call and the time and place of the meeting.

I. Real estate or other property may be acquired by purchase, gift, devise, or otherwise by local churches. Where real or personal property is acquired by deed, the instrument of conveyance shall contain the following clause, to wit:

"The said property is held in trust for the use and benefit of the members of the Church of God in Christ with National Headquarters in the city of Memphis, Shelly County, Tennessee, and the subject to the Charter, Constitution, Laws and Doctrine of said Church, now in full force and effect, or as they may be hereafter amended, changed or modified by the General Assembly of said Church."

J. The officers and trustees of a local church shall not mortgage church property in order to pay or meet current expenses of the church.

K. No deed, conveyance, or mortgage of real estate of a local church shall be binding on the Church of God in Christ unless the execution of said instrument has been approved in writing by the jurisdictional bishop having jurisdiction over the said local church.
L. Trustees, deacons, and other officers of a local church shall make an annual report to the congregation thereof.
M. A member of a local church may be licensed by his pastor to preach.
N. A licensed minister of a local church shall be ordained by the following procedures:
   1. He must first be recommended by his pastor to the ordination committee of the ecclesiastical jurisdiction of which his church is an affiliate, and the said pastor shall present the credentials and qualifications of the candidate to said committee.
   2. The credentials and qualifications of the candidate shall include his moral, spiritual fitness and attested loyalty to the church, and he shall also be required to satisfactorily complete a prescribed course of study as recognized by the jurisdictional assembly.
   3. If the committee approves the application of the candidate after examination and investigation of his credentials and qualifications, the candidate shall be recommended for ordination to his jurisdictional bishop.
   4. If the bishop approves, he shall thereupon ordain the applicant, who thereby becomes an ordained elder of the church.

O. Only an ordained elder may administer the ordinance of the church.
P. All credentials and certificates shall be uniform and shall be issued by the jurisdictional secretary.
Q. All vacancies that occur in the pastorate of a local church shall be filled by the jurisdictional bishop. The supervision and management of the church shall remain with the jurisdictional bishop or his designee until such time as a pastor is appointed to fill such vacancy.
R. No local church shall be authorized to change or transfer its jurisdictional affiliation unless two-thirds (2/3) of the church's membership agrees to such transfer. Two-thirds of the membership must be present and

voting after due notice before authorization can be given to move the church from one jurisdiction to another.

1. The pastor of the church shall notify in writing the jurisdictional secretary of the Church of God in Christ, the jurisdictional bishop where the church is affiliated, and the jurisdictional bishop where the church intends to transfer; of the intent to transfer, which notice shall be given at least thirty (30) days before the local church's membership can act on the said transfer. The notice shall include the following information:
   a. Name of pastor
   b. Name and location of the church
   c. Membership enrollment
   d. Jurisdiction where church is affiliated
   e. Name and address of jurisdictional bishop
   f. Jurisdiction where church seeks to transfer and name of bishop of such jurisdiction

2. The respective jurisdictional bishop or his designee where the church is affiliated and where the church seeks to transfer shall be entitled to be present at the membership meeting convened for this purpose.
3. The vote on the transfer shall be by secret ballot. The respective jurisdictional bishops shall be authorized to have a representative present to observe the voting and the counting of the ballots.
4. The respective jurisdictional bishop and the pastors of the local church shall, within seventy-two (72) hours, notify the general secretary of the Church of God in Christ of the results.

S. No local church shall be authorized to petition for a transfer of its jurisdictional affiliations but for one time each twelve-month period.

T. A member of a local church shall not transfer membership to another local Church of God in Christ unless the local member has the written consent of the pastor where the members enrolled. The pastor should give the member who is in good standing a letter of consent upon request.

ARTICLE VI. CHURCH DISCIPLINE

I. TRIALS OF LOCAL CHURCHES

A. Offenses for which a church may be tried are as follows.
   1. Persistently violating the provisions of the charter, constitution and rules, laws and regulations of the Church of God in Christ or its articles of faith
   2. Sustaining and supporting a pastor who teaches or practices doctrines contrary or repugnant to the articles of faith of the Church of God in Christ
   3. Sanctioning immoral practices of members and failing or refusing to take steps prescribed by the constitution and bylaws of the church for trial of members charged with the commission of the foregoing offenses

B. Procedure for Trial

   1. Any member of a local church who has just cause to believe that the church of which he is a member of has committed any or all of the offenses enumerated hereinabove may file a charge against the church, specifically setting out the acts and things complained about. The original charge shall be filed in the office of the secretary of the ecclesiastical jurisdiction of which the church is a part or with which it is affiliated, and copies thereof shall be filed with the clerk or secretary of the local church and in the office of the general secretary.
   2. The clerk of the ecclesiastical jurisdiction shall submit the charge to the jurisdictional bishop, who shall appoint an investigating committee of not less than three (3) or more than five (5) members to examine the facts and ascertain whether there is reasonable ground for having the church brought to trial.
   3. The investigating committee shall report its findings and recommendations to the jurisdictional bishop. If the investigating committee determines that there is no merit to the charge and

recommends that the charge be dismissed, the jurisdictional bishop shall thereupon dismiss the charge and send copies of the letter or order of dismissal to the principal parties.
4. If, however, the investigating committee determines that the church should be tried, it shall submit its recommendations to the jurisdictional bishop, who shall appoint an ecclesiastical council consisting of five (5) pastors of the jurisdiction to determine the merits of the complaint. The said council shall give written notice to all interested parties and to the jurisdictional secretary of the time and place of the hearing at least twenty (20) days prior to the time the ecclesiastical council sets the cause down for trial.
5. The parties shall have the right to be represented by counsel, who shall be members of the Church of God in Christ, but the said counsel may be advised by nonmembers of the church.
6. The majority decision of the ecclesiastical council shall be necessary to sustain the charge.
7. In the event the charges are not sustained, the complaint shall be dismissed. But if the charges are sustained, the council shall render its judgment or decision as follows:
   a. It may order that the church be placed on probation; or
   b. It may order or recommend that the church be given an opportunity to repent for its evil ways, agree to conform to the government and faith of the church, recognize the constitutional authorities of the church, and specifically refrain from committing, in the future, any of the acts embraced in the charges; or
   c. It may order that the church reorganize; or
   d. It may order that the church be disorganized; or
   e. It may order that the pastor be suspended or removed from office; or
   f. It may make such other orders or decisions as it may determine to be for the best interest of the Church of God in Christ.

8. The jurisdictional bishop shall execute the orders and decrees of the ecclesiastical council.

9. If and in the event a church is disorganized, its property—real and personal—shall pass to the trustees of the ecclesiastical assembly; and the officers of the said church, or trustees thereof, who have the legal right to convey title shall execute a deed of conveyance wherein the legal title to the said property shall be vested in the trustees of the ecclesiastical assembly, in trust, for the use and benefit of the members of the Church of God in Christ in the ecclesiastical jurisdiction of the church. But the said trustees shall not dispose of said property, except by and with the written consent of the jurisdictional bishop and the trustees of the general church.

II. TRIALS OF PASTORS OF LOCAL CHURCHES

A. A pastor may be tried for the commission of the following offenses, to wit:

1. Repeated failure to abide by the laws, rules, and regulations the Church of God in Christ
2. Misfeasance, malfeasance, or nonfeasance in office
3. Conviction of a felony or misdemeanor involving moral turpitude in a court of law
4. Espousing doctrines repugnant to the articles of faith of the Church of God in Christ
5. Personal misconduct
6. Misappropriation or misuse of the funds of the church
7. Conduct unbecoming a minister of the Gospel

B. The procedure for the trial of a local pastor shall be as follows:

1. When majority of the members of the Church of God in Christ have documented evidence that a pastor of a local church has committed any or all of the offenses enumerated hereinabove, they may file charges against such pastor, specifically setting out the acts and things complained about. The original copy of the charges shall be filed in the office of the general secretary of the assembly

of the ecclesiastical jurisdiction of which the church and pastor are a part or with which they are affiliated, and copies thereof shall be filed in the office of the general secretary of the Church of God in Christ at its national headquarters in Memphis, Tennessee.

2. The clerk of the assembly of the said ecclesiastical jurisdiction shall submit the charges to the jurisdictional bishop, who shall appoint an investigation committee of not less than three (3) or more than five (5) members to examine the facts and ascertain whether there are reasonable grounds for having the pastors brought to trail.

3. The investigation committee shall report its findings and recommendations to the jurisdictional bishop, and if it reports that the charges are without merit, the same shall be dismissed by the jurisdictional bishop, and notice of the dismissal shall be sent to all interested parties, including the general secretary.

4. If the investigating committee finds and determines that the pastor should be tried, it shall submit its recommendations to the jurisdictional bishop, who shall refer the case to the elders' council of the respective ecclesiastical jurisdiction; and the secretary of the elders' council shall give written notice to all principal parties; and a copy of said notices shall also be filed in the office of the general secretary at the national headquarters in Memphis, Tennessee; and said notices shall be given at least twenty (20) days prior to the time the elders' council shall set the matter down for trial.

5. The parties shall have the right to be represented by counsel, who shall be members of the Church of God in Christ, but the said counsel may be advised by nonmembers of the church.

6. Decisions of the members of the elders' council by a majority vote shall be necessary to sustain the charges and find the pastor guilty of committing the alleged offenses.

7. In the event the charges are not sustained, the complaint shall be dismissed. But if the charges are sustained, it shall render its decision or enter a decree as follows:
    a. It may occur that the pastor be placed on probation; or
    b. It may suspend the pastor for a definite period of time; or

    c. It may remove him from office and declare the pulpit vacant; or
    d. It may render such other decisions or decrees as justice may demand or as it may determine to be for the best interest of the Church of God in Christ.

8. In the event a pastor is dissatisfied with the decision or decree of the jurisdictional elders' council, he may appeal to the general council by filing notice of appeal with the secretary thereof within thirty (30) days from the final decision of the elders' council of the respective jurisdiction.
9. The general council shall review the case and render its decision by a majority vote of the delegates and members present and voting.
10. The jurisdictional bishop shall execute the orders and decrees of the general council.

III. TRIALS OF JURISDICTIONAL OFFICERS

A. The trial of jurisdictional officers, except jurisdictional bishops, shall be the same in all respects as that of a pastor.

ARTICLE VII. JUDICIARY COMMITTEE

I. THE JUDICIARY COMMITTEE
II. JUDICIAL ADMINISTRATION

ARTICLE VIII. JURISDICTIONAL CONVENTIONS

A. Jurisdictional conventions shall consist of one convocation, one Spring Workers' Meeting.
B. There shall be one district meeting per year, per district.
C. The following departments shall have one convention/conference per year.
    1. Jurisdictional Women's Department
    2. Jurisdictional Sunday School

3. Jurisdictional Youth Department
4. Jurisdictional Music Department
5. Jurisdictional Evangelist Department
6. Jurisdictional Missions Department
7. Jurisdictional Usher Department

All jurisdictional conferences, conventions, or meetings shall convene and terminate at the discretion of the bishop.

ARTICLE IX. PARLIAMENTARIAN AUTHORITY

The assembly of First Jurisdiction—Illinois Church of God in Christ shall be governed by the constitution in its deliberations. Where the constitution and the assembly rules are silent, the *Robert Rules of Order* newly revised (ninth) edition shall be followed.

Article X. Amendment to the Constitution

The provisions of this constitution may be modified, altered, or amended by a two-third (2/3) majority vote of all registered and certified delegates present and voting at a meeting of the assembly of First Jurisdiction—Illinois Church of God in Christ. As soon as the proposed alterations or amendments shall have been adopted as herein provided, the results of the date shall be announced by the secretary of the jurisdictional assembly and declared adopted by the chairman, whereupon such alterations or amendments shall be in full force and affect.

HANDOUT NO. 4

THE JURISDICTIONAL BUDGET MANUAL

CHURCH OF GOD IN CHRIST

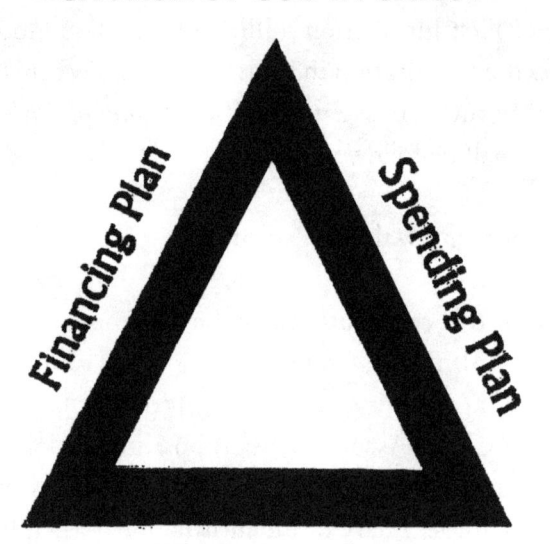

Financing Plan

Spending Plan

Ministry Plan

The Jurisdictional Budget Manual

JURISDICTIONAL BUDGET MANUAL DEVELOPERS

Superintendent Thomas Jackson Jr.

First Jurisdiction—Illinois

Missionary Dorothy Brown, Esq., CPA

First Jurisdiction—Illinois

Superintendent Isaiah Grover

First Jurisdiction—Illinois

PREFACE

THIS PUBLICATION IS about the jurisdictional budget plan and the role it plays in the jurisdictional management process. The task of operating a jurisdiction of the Church of God in Christ is a huge one. It involves many types of ministry activities that should be a part of the jurisdiction's budget.

A budget helps provide the answers to two basic questions—"How are we doing?" and "Where are we going?" It is obvious that a budget is not and cannot be a substitute for management itself.

For the many dollars spent annually in support of a jurisdiction, safeguards must be established and utilized from the time the monies are received until the time of proper disbursement. A budget must be carefully prepared so as to provide for the needs of a well-balanced ministry. In addition, an efficient fiscal procedure should be established whereby financial transactions are properly accounted for in a manner that simplifies subsequent auditing.

The budget needs of various jurisdictions differ yet have a good deal in common. The budget needs of various jurisdictions differ because mission statements differ. Mission statements differ because of varying sizes, methods of organization, geographical locations, states of development, different technical specialization of the members, etc. At the same time, jurisdictions have much in common because the main mission of all jurisdictions is to *reach the lost at any cost*, and the underlying questions that must be answered are the same.

Effort has been made to organize this budget manual logically. Sample forms included are designed to help the jurisdiction through the budgeting process. The forms should, however, be adjusted to fit the needs of each jurisdiction. This manual shows how to use the budget and to define positive goals through the ministries.

In the last analysis, the usefulness of the budget is a function of quality, quantity, suitability, and the jurisdiction's willingness and ability to properly use it. It is hoped that this manual will help the bishop to effectively direct the jurisdiction toward the mission set forth.

Obviously, each basic subject in a budget cannot be covered in detail here; however, it is hoped that the user will gain insights and leads to better understand the budgetary process. Much of the information and interpretation in this budget manual come from consultations and interviews with bishops, jurisdictional officials, and corporate specialists.

The authors of this publication owe a debt of gratitude to former presiding bishop Chandler D. Owens, whose "Vision 2000" was a motivating factor in stimulating good leadership into action.

The editor is grateful to the several contributors whose collective input allowed us to prepare a stronger issue than could have been achieved by any single individual.

> Superintendent Thomas Jackson Jr.
> Chicago, Illinois—Revised 2007

CONTENTS

PREFACE 97
INTRODUCTION 103
THE JURISDICTIONAL BUDGETARY PROCESS SUMMARY 109
THE JURISDICTIONAL BUDGETARY PROCESS GENERAL
    INFORMATION 111
BUDGET BY MINISTRY 117
    Consolidating Budget by Ministry 117
    Consolidated Budget by Ministry 119
RECOMMENDED DAY-TO-DAY ACCOUNTING
    PROCEDURES AND REPORTING 129

EXHIBIT

    BUDGET-PROCESS FORMS
    Exhibit A—Consolidating Budget by Ministry 117
    Exhibit B—Consolidated Budget by Ministry 119
    Exhibit C—Consolidating Jurisdictional Budget 119
    Exhibit D—Consolidated Jurisdictional Budget 122
    Exhibit E—Consolidated Jurisdictional Budget Summary by Ministry 125

    DAY-TO-DAY ACCOUNTING PROCEDURES AND RECORDING
    Exhibit F—Cash Receipts Report Form 131
    Exhibit G—Expenditure Requisition Form 132
    Exhibit H—Check Request Form 133
    Exhibit I—Expenditure Reimbursement Form 134
    Exhibit J—Petty Cash Reimbursement Form 135
    Exhibit K—Financial Performance Report 136

JURISDICTIONAL BUDGET MANUAL

INTRODUCTION

THIS JURISDICTIONAL BUDGET manual is intended to provide guidance in the development of an annual budget. It identifies several basic areas of jurisdiction business administration, presenting budgeting principles and good business practices and procedures.

The jurisdictional budget must be carefully prepared so as to provide for the operating needs of the jurisdiction as well as the jurisdictional ministries. This manual demonstrates the tools necessary to design a jurisdictional budget and control jurisdictional funds. Following the guidelines in this manual will aid a jurisdiction in its efforts to maximize its return through its ministries.

In addition to having a jurisdictional budget, safeguards must be established so that funds are properly controlled from the time of receipt to the time of disbursement. An efficient fiscal procedure should be established so that all financial transactions are properly accounted for in a manner that will simplify subsequent auditing. This manual will also recommend procedures for controlling the receipt and disbursement of jurisdictional funds.

Periodic financial reports must be compiled to provide the jurisdictional leadership with the information essential for proper control and future planning.

The *jurisdictional budget* may be defined as "a complete financial forecast of both receipts and expenditures, and includes both operating and capital budgets." An operating budget includes the proposed expenditures related to operating a jurisdiction on a day-to-day basis and how to purchase assets with useful lives of less than a year and the related funding. A capital budget includes the proposed expenditures related to the purchase of assets with useful lives of more than a year such as church buildings, organ, buses, etc., and the related funding.

The ideal jurisdictional budget should contain three parts:

1. The ministry plan—a definite statement of the ministerial goals and the programs that the jurisdiction will implement to meet those goals.
2. The spending plan—this is a translation of the ministerial goals into the proposed expenditures necessary to achieve the goals through the designated programs.
3. The financing plan—this is the proposed means of raising funds to finance the programs designed to achieve the ministerial goals.

The ministry plan must be the first plan developed since it forms the basis for the spending and financing plans. The three plans are closely integrated. An equilateral triangle symbolizes the ideal budget as indicated below:

Financing Plan

Spending Plan

Ministry Plan

The triangular plan is the only logical approach to the development of a jurisdictional budget since it emphasizes the fact that the ministry plan desired should be determined before the costs are calculated.

The jurisdictional budget is not a substitute for good, sound business administration. The budget is only to assist the administration. It is important that there are proper controls in place to ensure compliance with the budget, but the budget should not be followed blindly. The budgetary process should provide for necessary amendments throughout the year to meet the jurisdiction's ministerial goals.

The jurisdictional budget serves practical purposes:

1. The Budget Is a Servant of Ministry

    The jurisdiction does not exist in order to serve a budget; the budget is the servant, and the ministry is the master. The budget is a means and not an end.

2. The Budget Gives an Overview

    The budget functions directly in giving the jurisdiction officials an overview of the entire jurisdictional operations. It affords the jurisdiction the means of seeing the ministry, spending, and financing plans as an entity.

3. The Budget Aids in Analysis

    The budget also operates as a microscope in the analysis of details. Preparation of the annual budget should be accompanied by a critical evaluation of new ministries.

4. The Budget Develops Cooperation within the Jurisdiction

    A well-developed procedure for developing and administering the budget leads toward cooperation within the jurisdiction. Persons in charge of the business activities learn much about ministry requirements, and similarly, members of the ministry staff become better acquainted with some of the intricacies of financing the ministry plan.

5. The Budget Stimulates Confidence among the Pastors

   When a jurisdiction has a well-developed budget, pastors will be stimulated to support the ministry with financial support.

6. The Budget Improves the Accounting Procedures

   Where the budget is woven into the accounting system, there is a mutual interdependence. It has items accurately classified under appropriate headings with corresponding similar divisions in the accounting books. A good budget cannot function properly without a correspondingly good system of accounting.

7. The Budget Aids in Additional Outreach Ministries

   As jurisdictional ministries increase, there is the need for administrative control. Each organizational unit should be required to prepare a budget and a working plan for the next year.

8. The Budget Projects the Jurisdiction into the Future

   By planning ahead for a period of twelve months, the budget calls for extensive financial and programmatic forecasting. It involves a forward look in the means to accomplish the ministry plan.

THE JURISDICTIONAL BUDGETARY PROCESS SUMMARY

THE FOUR MAJOR steps in jurisdictional budgeting are

1. preparation,
2. presentation and adoption,
3. administration, and
4. appraisal.

Each of the four major phases is discussed briefly in the order indicated.

I. Preparation

  A. Ministry Plan Meeting

   The bishop, the board of directors, superintendents prepare, with staff and department-head assistance, a ministry plan on which the budgeted estimates are to be based.

   1. The bishop appoints a jurisdictional budget committee and calls for the budget.

B. Budget by Ministry Meeting (exhibits A and B)

    The jurisdictional budget committee requests from each ministerial unit heads a written ministry plan and budget and, after review, give preliminary approval.

C. The jurisdictional budget committee prepares and presents the preliminary jurisdictional budget to the bishop and the board of directors for approval (exhibits C and D).

II. PRESENTATION AND ADOPTION

A. The preliminary jurisdictional budget is presented to the bishop and jurisdiction assembly for adoption (exhibit E).
B. After formal adoption, the budget estimates are given to the jurisdictional budget committee for completion.

III. ADMINISTRATION

A. The completed budget estimates are given to the accounting department for final preparation and distribution.
B. The budget functions as a guide for the economical and efficient administration of the jurisdiction.

IV. APPRAISAL

A. The close of the fiscal year calls for an independent audit of the accounts and a critical appraisal of the administration of the jurisdiction's program; these are the two bases on which the succeeding year's budget is built.

THE JURISDICTIONAL BUDGETARY PROCESS
GENERAL INFORMATION

THE JURISDICTIONAL BUDGET shall consist of the following:

- A consolidating budget by ministry
- A consolidated budget by ministry
- A consolidating jurisdictional budget
- A consolidated jurisdictional budget
- A consolidated jurisdictional budget summary by ministry

The following pages describe the preparation process for each of these budgets.

The Call for a Budget

The jurisdictional budget should be prepared annually. The budget should be requested by the jurisdictional bishop in writing by a date as set by the jurisdictional calendar. The jurisdictional bishop must include in his request any new program for all ministries as agreed to with the jurisdictional ministry heads in the "ministry plan" meeting. The request for budget preparation will be made to the jurisdictional budget committee.

The jurisdictional budget committee will request in writing a budget for each ministry—i.e., the bishop's office, the staff supervisor's office, the general operations of the jurisdiction, the departments/auxiliaries, and all other ministries of the jurisdiction (each of these shall be referred to as a "ministry").

The jurisdictional budget committee will establish the budget calendar indicating due dates for submission, review, approval and forward it along with the written call for a budget to the appropriate parties. The committee will also provide each ministry head with a copy of the financial results of the ministry from the prior year. The jurisdictional budget committee will ensure that a balanced budget has been prepared by the jurisdictional bishop by December 31 of each year.

SUGGESTED BUDGET CALENDAR

June	• Ministry plan meeting with ministry heads	I PREPARATION
August	• Bishop's request for jurisdictional budget • Jurisdictional budget committee requests for each ministry's budget	
October	• Ministry budget submission, preparation, and preliminary approval by jurisdictional budget committee	
November	• Preliminary jurisdictional budget preparation by the jurisdictional budget committee • Presentation of preliminary jurisdictional budget to bishop and board of directors	II PRESENTATION AND ADOPTION
	• Approval by bishop and jurisdictional assembly of jurisdictional budget	
December	• Preparation of final jurisdictional budget and distribution • Call for independent audit and critical appraisal of ministry programs	III ADMINISTRATION

EXHIBIT

BUDGET-PROCESS FORMS

EXHIBIT A

SAMPLE JURISDICTION MINISTRY_____ CONSOLIDATING BY MINISTRY FOR YEAR ENDING	\multicolumn{8}{c	}{MINISTRIES}	
	President	Chair-lady	Monthly Meeting	Annual Meeting	Banquets/ Luncheons	Outreach Ministries	Workshops and Seminars	Other	TOTALS
REVENUES									
Public Offering									
Monthly Reports—Leaders									
Monthly Reports—Churches									
Bishop's Offering									
State Supervisor's Offering									
District Reports									
Licensed Officials' Reports									
Woman of the Year Event									
Women's Convention									
Tithing									
Interest									
Missions									
Banquets/Luncheons, etc.									
Other Ministries' Income									
Other Income:									
TOTAL REVENUES									

EXPENDITURES

Annual Breakfast								
Annual Dinner								
Audit and Accounting								
Automobile Expenses								
Bank Charges								
Support of Individual Churches								
Clerical								
Equipment Rental								
Grants/Scholarships								
Honorariums								
Insurance Health/ Property								
Legal Services								
Maintenance/Repairs								
Meeting/Seminar/ Conference								
Office Supplies								
Outreach Ministry								
Payroll Taxes								
Photographer								
Postal								
Printing								
Public Relations								
Purchase of Capital Items								
Salaries and Wages								
Security								
Travel								
Trophies/Awards								
Utilities								
Other Expenditure								
TOTAL EXPENDITURE								

REVENUE OVER/ UNDER EXPENDITURES								

EXHIBIT C

MINISTRIES

SAMPLE JURISDICTION CONSOLIDATING JURISDICTIONAL BUDGET FOR YEAR ENDING _____	Bishop	State Supervisor	Board of Directors	Operation and Administration	Workers Meeting	Convocation	Pastor and Elder's Council	Women's Department	YPWW	AIM	Sunday School	Music Department	Missions	Evangelist	Scholastic Motivation	TOTALS
REVENUES																
Public Offering																
Monthly Reports—Leaders																
Monthly Reports—Churches																
Bishop's Offering																
State Supervisor's Offering																
District Reports																
Licensed Officials Reports																
Woman of the Year Event																
Women's Convention																
Tithing																
Interest																
Missions																
Banquet/ Luncheons, etc.																
Capital Items Funding																
Other Ministries Income																
Other Income:																
TOTAL REVENUE																

EXPENDITURES

- Annual Breakfast
- Annual Dinner
- Audit and Accounting
- Automobile Expenses
- Bank Charges
- Support of Individual Churches
- Clerical
- Equipment Rental
- Grants/ Scholarships
- Honorariums
- Insurance Health/ Property
- Legal Services
- Maintenance/ Repairs
- Meeting/Seminar/ Conference
- Office Supplies
- Outreach Ministry
- Payroll Taxes
- Photographer
- Postal
- Printing
- Public Relations
- Purchase of Capital Items
- Salaries and Wages
- Security
- Travel
- Trophies/Awards
- Utilities
- Other Expenditures
- TOTAL EXPENDITURES
- REVENUES OVER/UNDER EXPENDITURES

CONSOLIDATED JURISDICTIONAL BUDGET

DESCRIPTION

The consolidated jurisdictional budget shall be prepared by the jurisdictional budget committee. The consolidated jurisdictional budget will consist of the grand total of all of the jurisdictional budget committee preliminary approved ministry budgets as shown in the last column of the consolidating jurisdictional budget.

The jurisdictional budget committee shall prepare the consolidated jurisdictional budget using the consolidating jurisdictional budget. The jurisdictional budget committee shall prepare the consolidated jurisdictional budget by the date set by the budget calendar.

EXHIBIT D

Consolidated Jurisdictional Budget for the Year Ending

SAMPLE JURISDICTION

BUDGETED AMOUNT

REVENUES

Public Offering	
Monthly Reports—Leaders	
Monthly Reports—Churches	
Bishop's Offering	
State Supervisor's Offering	
District Reports	
Licensed Officials' Reports	
Woman of the Year Event	
Women's Convention	
Tithing	
Interest	
Missions	
Banquets/Luncheons, etc.	
Other Ministries' Income	
Other Income:	
TOTAL REVENUES	

EXPENDITURES

Annual Breakfast	
Annual Dinner	
Audit and Accounting	

Automobile Expenses	
Bank Charges	
Support of Individual Churches	
Clerical	
Equipment Rental	
Grants/Scholarships	
Honorariums	
Insurance Health/Property	
Legal Services	
Maintenance/Repairs	
Meeting/Seminar/Conference	
Office Supplies	
Outreach Ministry	
Payroll Taxes	
Photographer	
Postal	
Printing	
Public Relations	
Purchase of Capital Items	
Salaries and Wages	
Security	
Travel	
Trophies/Awards	
Utilities	
Other Expenditures	
TOTAL EXPENDITURES	

REVENUES OVER/UNDER EXPENDITURES	

CONSOLIDATED JURISDICTIONAL BUDGET SUMMARY BY MINISTRY

DESCRIPTION

The consolidated jurisdictional budget summary by ministry shall be prepared by the jurisdictional budget committee. The consolidated jurisdictional budget summary will include the grand total of revenues and expenses for each ministry. There will be a line item under the revenues section for each ministry. The total budgeted revenues for each ministry, as shown on the budget by ministry, and the consolidating jurisdictional budget shall be shown for each ministry. The total budgeted expenses for each ministry, as shown on the budget by ministry, and the consolidating jurisdictional budget shall also be shown for each ministry.

The jurisdictional budget committee shall prepare the consolidated jurisdictional budget summary using the budget by ministry for each ministry and consolidating jurisdictional budget. The jurisdictional budget committee shall prepare the consolidated jurisdictional budget summary by the date set by the budget calendar.

EXHIBIT E

Consolidated Jurisdictional Budget Summary By Ministry

Sample Jurisdiction

FOR THE YEAR ENDING: _____

REVENUES	Consolidated Budget
Bishop	$ -
State Supervisor	$ -
Board of Directors	$ -
Operations and Administration	$ -
Workers' Meeting	$ -
Convocation	$ -
Pastors' and Elders' Council	$ -
Women's Department	$ -
YFWW	$ -
Sunday School	$ -
AIM	$ -
Music Department	$ -
Missions	$ -
Evangelist	$ -
Capital Items	$ -
Scholastic Motivation	$ -
TOTAL REVENUES	$ -

EXPENDITURES	
Bishop	$ -
State Supervisor	$ -
Board of Directors	$ -
Operations and Administration	$ -
Workers' Meeting	$ -
Convocation	$ -
Pastors' and Elders' Council	$ -
Women's Department	$ -
YFWW	$ -
Sunday School	$ -
AIM	$ -
Music Department	$ -
Missions	$ -
Evangelist	$ -
Capital Items	$ -
Scholastic Motivation	$ -
TOTAL REVENUES	$ -
REVENUE OVER/UNDER EXPENDITURES	

DAY-TO-DAY ACCOUNTING PROCEDURES AND RECORDING

RECOMMENDED DAY-TO-DAY ACCOUNTING PROCEDURES AND REPORTING

Revenues

All cash collected by a ministry will be submitted immediately to the treasurer of the jurisdiction. A cash receipts report form, three-part form (exhibit F), will be used to submit the funds. The form must be approved by the ministry head. The ministry head and the treasurer must agree upon the amount submitted, and then the treasurer must sign the form as evidence of receipt. A copy of the signed form should be given to the ministry head to be maintained in the ministry's records; a copy should be maintained by the treasurer, and a copy should be forwarded to the jurisdictional budget committee for the jurisdiction's records.

Expenditures

Request to spend money out of a budget will be made using an expenditure requisition form (exhibit G). The expenditure requisition form must be preapproved by the jurisdictional budget committee.

This form must be pre-approved whether a jurisdictional check is to be used to prepay the amount or if the amount is going to be reimbursed. If a jurisdictional check is to be used to purchase the item, then a check request form (exhibit H) must also be submitted with the requisition form. Invoices or quotes, where available, should accompany the check request form. Original receipts should be submitted after the purchase has been made. The expenditure requisition form and the check request form must be approved by the ministry head and the jurisdictional budget committee.

If the expenditure is to be reimbursed, then an expenditure reimbursement form (exhibit I), along with the original receipt(s), must be approved by the ministry head and submitted to the jurisdictional budget committee for approval. Only expenditures with approved expenditure requisition forms on file will be reimbursed.

Petty Cash Fund

A petty cash fund in the amount of $_____ (established by jurisdiction) should be established for each ministry. The ministry head should maintain the fund in a bank account. Receipts for purchases made from the fund should be kept and submitted, along with a petty cash reimbursement form (exhibit J), to the jurisdictional budget committee for reimbursement of the fund. Only the type of expenses previously approved in the budget should be purchased from these funds. No item costing more than $_____ (established by the jurisdiction) should be purchased using these funds. All purchases from this fund should be approved by the ministry head.

Performance Reports

A quarterly performance report must be submitted to the jurisdictional budget committee on the performance report form (exhibit K). The report must show the actual budget and variation from the budget. All expenses over the budget must be explained. This report must also include ministry accomplishments for the quarter.

An annual performance report must be submitted to the jurisdictional budget committee on the performance report form (exhibit K). This report must also include ministry accomplishments for the year.

EXHIBIT F

Cash Receipts Report Form

Sample Jurisdiction

Submitting Ministry _____   Receipt Date _____

Description	Amount
Total	

Approvals

Ministry Head* _____
                         Signature   Date

Treasurer* _____
                         Signature   Date

*   Indicates that the total amount submitted has been agreed by the ministry head and treasurer

EXHIBIT G

Expenditure Requisition Form

Sample Jurisdiction

Requesting Ministry:_____
Request Date:_____

Budgeted Line Item Description: _____
Amount: _____

Item Description	Quantity	Price	Amount
TOTAL REQUISITION			
TOTAL BUDGET TO DATE BEFORE REQUISITION			
TOTAL BUDGET TO DATE, INCLUDING THE REQUISITION			

REQUISITION NO. _____

Approvals

Ministry Head _____
                        Signature   Date

JBC Representative _____
                        Signature   Date

Invoices or quotes should be submitted.

EXHIBIT H

Check Request Form

Sample Jurisdiction

Requesting Ministry:_____
Request Date:_____

PAYEE: _____
NAME: _____
ADDRESS:_____

Item Description	Quantity	Price	Amount
	TOTAL		

REQUISITION NO. _____   CHECK NO. _____

Approvals

Ministry Head _____
                        Signature   Date

JBC Representative _____
                        Signature   Date

If this is for a reimbursement, then an expenditure reimbursement form, along with receipts, should also be submitted. If this is for an original purchase, then the receipts should be submitted to the JBC immediately upon purchase.

EXHIBIT I

Expenditure Reimbursement Form

Sample Jurisdiction

Requesting Ministry:_____
Request Person:_____
Date:_____
Requisition No._____

(An expenditure request form must be on file for reimbursement.)

Item Description	Quantity	Price	Amount
	TOTAL		

* Attach all original receipts.

Approvals

Ministry Head* _____
                              Signature   Date

Treasurer* _____
                              Signature   Date

Note: A check request form should also be prepared.

EXHIBIT J

Petty Cash Reimbursement Form

Sample Jurisdiction

Requesting Ministry:_____
Request Date:_____

LIST OF EXPENDITURES	
Item Description	Amount
TOTAL REIMBURSEMENT REQUEST	
TOTAL CURRENTLY IN FUND	
TOTAL PETTY CASH FUND	

Approvals

Ministry Head _____
                        Signature   Date

JBC Representative _____
                        Signature   Date

EXHIBIT K

Financial Performance Report

Sample Jurisdiction

For the _____ Months Ended through _____

	Actual	Budget to Date	Variance Over/Under Budget
REVENUES			
Public Offering			
Monthly Reports—Leaders			
Monthly Reports—Churches			
Bishop's Offering			
State Supervisor's Offering			
District Reports			
Licensed Officials' Reports			
Woman of the Year Event			
Women's Convention			
Tithing			
Interest			
Missions			
Banquets/Luncheons, etc.			
Other Ministries' Income			
Other Income:			
TOTAL REVENUES			

EXPENDITURES

Annual Breakfast			
Annual Dinner			
Audit and Accounting			
Automobile Expenses			
Bank Charges			
Support of Individual Churches			
Clerical			
Equipment Rental			

Grants/Scholarships			
Honorariums			
Insurance Health/Property			
Legal Services			
Maintenance/Repairs			
Meeting/Seminar/Conference			
Office Supplies			
Outreach Ministry			
Payroll Taxes			
Photographer			
Postal			
Printing			
Public Relations			
Purchase of Capital Items			
Salaries and Wages			
Security			
Travel			
Trophies/Awards			
Utilities			
Other Expenditures			
TOTAL EXPENDITURES			

REVENUES OVER/UNDER EXPENDITURES			

HANDOUT NO. 5

JUDICIARY BOARD

PREAMBLE: THE JUDICIARY BOARD

THE ESTABLISHMENT OF the judiciary board of the Church of God in Christ Inc. shall bring into existence a third branch of church government, which shall exist in conjunction with the two present branches of government: the executive branch and the legislative branch. This branch of government shall be established as both an ecclesiastical and appellate court, hearing disputes upon appeal from lower dispute-resolution forums in the church and serving as the ultimate authority on matters of constitutional interpretation. All former articles and charters inconsistent with this amendment are modified, amended, and hereby repealed. Article 8 upon adoption shall be effective immediately.

The establishment of the judiciary board creates within the church a three-branch system of government similar to the United States of America federal government. The three-branch system of the Church of God in Christ Inc. shall be, however, a modification of the federal system in that the system of checks and balances of the latter is different from the former. Under the church government, this system of checks and balances is evidenced by the fact that the judiciary board members are elected and retained in office by the legislative branch (the general assembly) and by the fact that the judiciary board's budget is approved by the executive branch (the general board). The judicial branch (the judiciary board) shall balance the legislative and executive branches by being a final authority on questions of constitutionality and the final appellate forum of the church for disputes.

Whereas there exists presently forums of dispute resolution within the church (e.g., the judiciary committee of the board of bishops, the judicial committee of the council of pastors and elders, and the dispute resolution forum of the Women's Department), these forums shall continue to attempt to mediate or adjudicate disputes. It is only after a decision has been rendered by one of these existing forums that an aggrieved person or body has the right to appeal to the judiciary board.

This independent, objective branch of church government shall have as its highest objective the protection of the rights of every member of the Church of God in Christ Inc. as set forth in the church constitution. The protection of those rights shall be without regard for official position or social station. Therefore, it shall be crucial that the judiciary board decisions are rendered without intimidation, coercion, or undue influence and that the members of the said board are fair, sober, objective, and seasoned in their decision making.

The judiciary board shall serve to prevent the intrusion of civil authorities into the affairs of the church whenever inevitable disputes shall arise. Generally, the secular legal system has been reticent to intervene in the internal affairs of any religious body, preferring that the said disputes are resolved internally. Where the decisions of the judiciary board have been made objectively, consistent with precedent setting resolutions or with reasonable grounds for modifying or overruling previous rulings or resolutions and in accordance with legitimate interpretation of the church's constitution, the civil court would not readily overturn the said decisions.

Furthermore, the judiciary board shall allow for the participation of representatives of all sectors of the church in the ultimate resolution of disputes. The board shall be comprised of nine members, designated in three categories: episcopal, ministerial, and general. Three members shall be jurisdictional bishops (episcopal), four members shall be elders other than bishops (ministerial), and two members shall be from the church at large (general). This means that it will be possible for laymen and laywomen to serve the church on the judiciary board, provided they meet all other qualifications. This shall continue the tradition of inclusion that has made this church great.

The establishment of the judiciary board shall assure that the legitimately aggrieved members of the Church of God in Christ Inc. are heard, that fairness prevails throughout the brotherhood, and that equal protection and due process are and continue to be the right of every church member.

ARTICLE VIII—JUDICIARY BOARD

There shall be established a judiciary board for the Church of God in Christ Inc. The judiciary board shall be both an ecclesiastical and appellate court.

COMPOSITION AND CRITERIA

The judiciary board shall be composed of nine (9) members, designated in three (3) categories: episcopal, ministerial, and general. Three (3) members shall be jurisdictional bishops (episcopal), three (3) members shall be elders other than bishops (ministerial), and three (3) members shall be from the church at large (general). Each member shall be at least forty-five years of age and an active member of the Church of God in Christ for not less than twenty (20) successive years, persons of mature judgment, proven ability, integrity, and knowledge on Church of God in Christ constitutional matters.

1. The board of bishops shall elect from among its membership four (4) candidates for nomination. This election shall take place at the board's annual meeting during the national convocation. The notice of election shall be given by the secretary of the board of bishops to all bishops within thirty (30) days prior to the election. The list of candidates nominated shall be submitted to the secretary of the general assembly.
2. The general council of pastors and elders shall elect four (4) candidates from its membership for nomination. This election shall take place at the annual meeting during the national convocation. The notice of election shall be given by the secretary of the general council to all pastors and elders within thirty (30) days prior to the election. The list of candidates shall be submitted to the secretary of the general assembly.
3. The general assembly shall nominate twelve (12) candidates, and the general board shall nominate three (3) candidates from the registered delegates present at its annual meeting, of which only

four (4) shall be selected by a standing vote. During the selection process, the fifteen (15) nominees shall stand before the assembly. This procedure shall identify the four nominees of the general assembly whose names shall be submitted to the secretary of the general assembly.
4. The general assembly secretary shall announce the nominees to the general assembly and submit those named to the Judiciary Qualifications and Nominations Committee.
5. Members of the judiciary board shall be elected by the general assembly.

ELECTION PROCEDURES

1. The nominating committee shall present to the general assembly a ballot listing the names of the twelve (12) screened and approved judiciary board candidates. The nine (9) candidates shall be elected in the following order: the three (3) candidates from the board of bishops receiving the most votes, the three (3) candidates from the council of pastors and elders receiving the most votes, and the three (3) candidates from the general assembly receiving the most votes.
2. At the first election under this provision, three of the nine judiciary board members shall serve a three-year term; three board members, a five-year term; and three members, a seven-year term. The terms shall be staggered in order to avoid the expiration of the terms of all elected board members simultaneously.
3. The chairman, the vice chairman, and the secretary shall be elected by the constituents of the judiciary board. The first term of said positions shall be seven years. All other board members' terms shall be staggered according to the numbers of votes received, i.e., the three candidates (out of the remaining six) receiving the highest number of votes shall receive the five-year terms, and three members receiving the lowest amount of votes shall receive the three-year terms.

JUDICIARY QUALIFICATIONS AND NOMINATIONS COMMITTEE

1. A standing committee on judiciary qualifications and nominations composed of nine (9) members in good standing in the general assembly shall be appointed by the chairman of the general assembly with the approval of the general assembly. Members of the committee shall serve for a term of four (4) years to run concurrently with the term of the chairman of the general assembly.
2. The committee shall review and screen credentials of all nominees and shall determine whether the qualifying criteria established by the general assembly have been met. If for justifiable reasons a

nominee is rejected by the committee and the rejection is sustained by the general assembly, the process contained in the nominating procedures shall be repeated. The committee shall submit all qualified nominees for each vacancy to the general assembly for consideration.

TERM OF OFFICE

1. A judiciary board member's term of office, with the exception of the initial staggered term, shall be seven (7) years. A member shall not be elected for more than two (2) terms and may not serve more than fourteen (14) years in office.
2. Continuance in office beyond the initial term is subject to the approval of the registered delegates present and voting the general assembly session preceding the expiration of the term of office. The approval of the delegates shall be required for the member's continuance in office for a second term. The assembly delegates shall, by a method designated by the general assembly, vote for retention in office.
3. A. A judiciary board member may be removed from office prior to the expiration of his term due to incapacitation incompetency or for the commission of acts in violation of the constitution of the Church of God in Christ.

B. Procedures for filing and handling charges.

1. A delegate in good standing of the Church of God in Christ having just cause to believe that a member of the judiciary board has committed an act repugnant to the constitution of the Church of God in Christ may file a charge.
    a. The written petition shall be filed in the office of the secretary of the general assembly, specifically setting out the charges and things complained about, and copies shall be filed with the secretary of the judiciary board.

b. Every petition shall be signed by the individual making the charge, whose address shall also be stated. His signature constitutes a certificate by him that to the best of his knowledge, information, and belief, there is good ground to support the charge and that the charge is not made for improper purpose, such as to harass.
c. For a willful violation of this requirement, a petitioner shall be subjected to appropriate disciplinary action.

2. The secretary of the general assembly shall submit the charge to the chairman of the general assembly, who shall appoint an investigating committee of not less than three (3) or more than five (5) members to examine the facts and ascertain whether there is reasonable ground for having the member brought to trial.
3. The investigating committee shall report its findings and recommendations to the chairman of the general assembly. If the investigating committee determines that there is no merit to the charge and recommends that the charge be dismissed, the chairman of the general assembly shall thereupon dismiss the charge and send copies of the letter or order of dismissal to the principal parties.
4. If, however, the investigating committee finds and determines that the member should be tried, it shall submit its recommendations to the chairman of the general assembly, who shall appoint a judicial council of the general assembly.
5. The judiciary board shall prescribe its own methods and procedures for carrying out its duties. Such procedures shall be filed with the general secretary of the Church of God in Christ and each jurisdictional bishop within thirty (30) days of their adoption.
6. The judiciary board shall, with the approval of the general assembly, prepare and keep in revision a judicial code that shall be an addendum to the constitution of the Church of God in Christ and shall include procedures for trials and redress in all church-related matter. Changes or modifications to the judicial code shall receive prior approval of the general assembly.

7. Executive clemency may be granted by a majority vote of the general board in matters of a disciplinary nature, but not matters of a constitutional nature.
8. The judiciary board shall submit an annual budget request to the board of trustees for inclusion in the general church budget. The judiciary board may not exceed its approved budget without prior approval of the general assembly or the general board when the general assembly is not in session.

LEGAL COUNSEL

The judiciary board shall appoint a chief counsel to advise the board on all matters of a legal nature. The chief counsel must be a member of the Church of God in Christ. He or she must present adequate documentation of legal credentials. The chief counsel shall not only be licensed to practice law in his state of residence but must also be licensed to practice law in the state of Tennessee or be associated with a law firm or person licensed to practice law in the state of Tennessee. The chief counsel may appoint associate counsel to assist, with the approval of the judiciary board.

DUTIES

1. The judiciary board shall determine the constitutionality of any act of the general assembly upon the appeal of the majority of that assembly.
2. The judiciary board shall determine the constitutionality of any act of the general board upon the appeal of the majority of that board.
3. The judiciary board shall determine the constitutionality of any act of a jurisdictional assembly or a jurisdictional bishop upon the appeal of the majority of the pastors of the jurisdiction.
4. The judiciary board shall decide any election dispute referred to it by the general assembly.
5. The judiciary board shall be the final appeal court for all matters arising under the church discipline.

6. The judiciary board shall receive cases referred by the general board, the board of bishops, the council of pastors and elders, or the general assembly.
7. The judiciary board may hear and determine an appeal of a bishop when taken from a decision of the trial court in his case, provided a bishop must make known to the board of bishops and to the judiciary board in writing, within thirty (30) days after a decision, his intention to make such an appeal; and any decision made by the board of bishops shall not become effective unless the decision of the board of bishops is sustained by the judiciary board.
8. A district superintendent, pastor, or elder shall have the right to appeal to the judiciary board in case of an adverse decision by the trial court only where he received punishment that includes suspension or removal from his office and/or church, provided that within thirty (30) days after the said adverse decision, he notifies the secretary of the last body to hear his case and the secretary of the judiciary board of his intention to appeal. Any decision made by the trial court shall not be effective unless the trial court's decision is sustained by the judiciary board.
9. National officers shall have the right to appeal to the judiciary board in case of an adverse decision by the general board only where he received punishment that includes suspension or removal from his office, provided that within thirty (30) days after said adverse decision, he notifies the secretary of the general board and the secretary of the judiciary board of his intention to appeal. The decision of the general board shall not become effective unless the general board's decision is sustained by the judiciary board.
10. A general board member shall have the right to appeal to the judiciary board from a decision of the trial court in his case, provided he make known to the trial court in his case and to the judiciary board, in writing, within thirty (30) days after a decision, his intention to make such an appeal. The judicial council of the general assembly shall be the trial court for the trial of any general board member. The procedures for the trial of a general board member shall be the same as the procedures for the trial of a

judiciary board member. Any decision made by the judicial council shall not become effective unless the judicial council's decision is sustained by the judiciary board.

11. The chairman of the general assembly shall have the right to appeal to the judiciary board in case of an adverse decision by the trial court in his case, provided he make known to the trial court and to the judiciary board, in writing, within thirty (30) days after the decision, his intention to make such an appeal. The judicial council of the general assembly shall be the trial court for the trial of the chairman, presided over by a temporary chairman elected by the general assembly. The procedures for the trial of the general assembly chairman shall be the same as the procedures for the trial of a judiciary board member. The decision of the judicial council shall not become effective unless the council's decision is sustained by the judiciary board.

12. The judiciary board shall receive all referrals or petitions made to it by any authorized person or body in accordance with this constitution, provided that it is in writing and shall state the names and addresses of disputants and have the signatures of the appellant or the presiding officers of the body making the referral.

13. The judiciary board, on all cases handled, shall file its written findings of facts and recommendations and/or decisions with the general secretary and the presiding officer of the body who made the referral, and copies of all shall be disseminated to all interested parties.

14. The findings of facts and conclusions of law will be made available to the public. However, for good cause shown, the judiciary board may limit the availability of any document in order to prevent disclosure of confidential information or that which justice requires to protect an individual from undue embarrassment or oppression.

15. The judiciary board members shall refrain from all conflicts of interest that shall affect their impartial conduct of duty.

JUDICIARY BOARD SUMMARY

Supt. Thomas Jackson

	SENDING HOUSE	ELECTED 1992	OFFICE	REAFFIRM 1995	REAFFIRM 1997	1999	2000	2001	NEW ELECTION 2002	NEW ELECTION 2004	NEW ELECTION 2006	REAFFIRM
T. D. IGLEHART	BD BISHOP	3	MEMBER	7	CHAPMAN—DECEASED			NESBITT	X-S. NESBITT 7			2009
JOS MAYFIELD	COUNCIL	3	MEMBER	7					X-T. HAMMONDS 7			2009
NAT. WELLS	BD BISHOP	3	MEMBER	7	N. WELLS TO GEN. BD. PERRY				X-PERRY 7			2009
JOHN BUTLER	COUNCIL	5	MEMBER		7					X J. CLEMMONS 7		2011
COR. RANGE	COUNCIL	5	MEMBER		7					X T. SWANN 7		2011
D. L. LINDSEY	GENERAL ASSEMBLY	5	MEMBER		7					X T. JACKSON 7		2011
T. L. WESTBROOK	BD BISHOP	7	CHAIRMAN			7					X L. THOMAS 7	2013
C. D. KINSEY	GENERAL ASSEMBLY	7	VICE			7	KINSEY—NCAPACITATED	B. J. WARREN			X 7	2013
H. J. WILLIAMS	GENERAL ASSEMBLY	7	SECRETARY			7					X V. SLACK 7	2013

Church of God in Christ: Leadership Guidebook for Ministers

WORKSHOP

Understanding the Church of God in Christ Judiciary Board
Presenter: Admin. Asst. Thomas Jackson Jr.

Article 8 of the Church of God in Christ Charter specifically gives the judiciary board the final authority on questions of ecclesiastical constitutional doctrine. This judiciary board is the final appellate forum of the church for disputes.

The goal of this workshop will be to give historical and informational insight on the powers and prerogatives of the judiciary board.

Below is an outline of topics to be covered.

I. Biblical Judiciary Systems
   A. Mosaic
   B. Sanhedrin

II. The Church of God in Christ Judiciary System
   A. Preamble
      - Composition and Election
      - Mandate
   B. Authority
   C. Appeals Process
   D. Hearing Procedure
   E. Code of Conduct/Duties
   F. Code of Judicial Conduct

   Rule 1. Integrity and independence of the judiciary board.
        2. Avoidance of the appearance of impropriety.
        3. Impartial performance of duties of office.
        4. Activities to improve the administration of justice.
        5. Political activity.
        6. Compliance with the code of judicial conduct is mandatory.

G. Rules for Counselors and Advisors Appearing before the Judiciary Board of the Church of God in Christ

- Preamble
- Rules for Counselors and Advisors
    1. Confidentiality of information
    2. Terminating representation
    3. Candor toward the judiciary board
    4. Fairness to opposing party

HANDOUT NO. 6

Four-Step Problem-Solving Approach

Facilitator: Administrative Assistant Thomas Jackson Jr.

I. PROBLEM DEFINITION (*Get the Facts*)
   A. Where are we?
   B. What are the issues?
   C. What are our strengths?
   D. What are our weaknesses?

II. CREATIVE SOLUTIONS TO PROBLEMS (*Weigh and Decide*)
   A. Enumerating the Facts
   B. Objectives and Costs
      1. Determine objective.
      2. Set short-range goals.
      3. Set long-range goals.
   C. Alternative Methods
   D. Roadblocks

III. TAKE ACTION
   A. Developing a Strategy
   B. Available Resources
   C. Timetable

IV. CHECK RESULTS
   A. Follow Up on Action
   B. Next Meeting

HANDOUT NO. 7

Procedures for Conducting a Jurisdictional Trial

1. First of all, the provisions of the constitution of the Church of God in Christ Inc.—as provided in article 8, section B—must be compiled within its entirety.

2. After the jurisdictional pastors' and elders' council receives the case on referral from the jurisdictional bishop, it becomes the sole responsibility of the jurisdictional council to conduct the trial.

3. Upon receipt of the referral from the jurisdictional bishop, the chairman of the jurisdictional pastors' and elders' council shall call a meeting of the full council.

4. At the meeting of the council, the council shall establish the ground rules for the trial and set the date, time, and place where the trial will be held.

5. The council shall give thirty (30) days' written notice of date, time, and place of the trial to all concerned persons.

6. The jurisdictional bishop shall appoint one (1) or more pastors and/or elders to prosecute the case (to present the evidence against the defendant).

7. Pursuant to article 8, section B, paragraph 2-1 of the constitution, the defendant has the right to be represented by counsel.

8. In jurisdictions where there are large numbers of pastors and elders, it may be advisable for the chairman of the council to appoint a *judicial review committee* of not less than nine (9) or more than fifteen (15) members who shall conduct the hearing or trial.

9. At the date, time, and place scheduled, the council shall proceed to hold the trial.

10. If the council finds the defendant guilty, it shall set the penalty as provided in article 8, section B, paragraph 2, g-1, 2, 3, and 4.

11. If the defendant is found guilty or innocent, the jurisdictional bishop shall execute the orders and decrees of the jurisdictional pastors' and elders' council.

12. In the event the jurisdictional pastors' and elders' council uses a judicial review committee to conduct the trial, the committee shall make its decision by majority vote of the members present and who participated in the trial hearings.

13. After the committee has completed its work, the chairman of the committee shall inform the chairman of the jurisdictional pastors' and elders' council of its findings.

14. The chairman of the council shall call the full council together to a hearing for the report.

15. The council shall approve or disapprove the committee's report by a majority vote of those members present and voting.

16. Any member of the jurisdictional pastors' and elders' council who serves on the investigating committee or as a prosecutor shall not have the right to vote on the guilt or innocence of the defendant.

17. If a defendant is found guilty and the penalty imposed removes him from his office as pastor or otherwise adversely affects his livelihood, he shall have the right to a stay of execution pending appeal.

Prepared by Supt. Talbert Swann, past chairman of the
Judiciary Review Committee, General Council of Pastors and Elders

SUMMARY OF
ARTICLE VIII, SECTION B

Trial Procedures for the Trial of a Local Pastor

Documented charges filed against a pastor must follow the following procedures:

1. The original copy of charges shall be filed in the office of the secretary of the jurisdictional assembly.
2. Copies of these charges shall be filed in the office of the general secretary of the national church in Memphis, Tennessee.
3. The jurisdictional clerk (secretary) shall submit the charges to the *jurisdictional bishop*, who shall appoint an investigating committee of not less than three (3) or more than five (5) members to examine the facts and ascertain whether there are reasonable grounds for trial.
4. The investigating committee shall report its findings and recommendations to the jurisdictional bishop.
   a. If it reports that the charges are without merit, the charges shall be dismissed by the jurisdictional bishop, and a notice of the dismissal shall be sent to all interested parties, including the general secretary in Memphis, Tennessee.
   b. If the investigating committee finds and determines that the pastor should be tried, it shall submit its recommendations to the jurisdictional bishop, who shall refer the case to the jurisdictional *pastors' and elders' council*, and the secretary of the council shall give written notice to all principal parties. A copy of the said notices shall also be filed in the office of the national general secretary in Memphis, Tennessee. These notices shall be given at least twenty (20) days prior to the time the council set the matter down for trial.
   c. The parties shall have the right to be represented by counsel, who shall be members of the Church of God in Christ, but the said counsel may be advised by nonmembers of the church.

d. Decisions of the members of the jurisdictional council by a majority vote shall be necessary to sustain the charges and find the pastor guilty of committing the alleged offenses.
e. In the event the charges are not sustained, the complaint shall be dismissed.
f. If the charges are sustained, the council shall render its decision or enter a decree as follows:
    1. It may order that the pastor be placed on probation, or
    2. It may suspend the pastor for a definite period of time, or
    3. It may remove the pastor from office and declare the pulpit vacant, or
    4. It may render such other decisions or decrees as justice may demand or as it may determine to be in the best interest of the Church of God in Christ.

g. In the event a pastor is dissatisfied with the decision or decree of the jurisdictional pastors' and elders' council, he may appeal to the National General Council by filing a notice of appeal within thirty (30) days from the final decision of the jurisdictional pastors' and elders' council.

SUMMARY

Article VIII, Section B

Offenses for Which a Pastor May Be Tried

A pastor may be tried for the commission of the following offenses:

1. Repeated failure to abide by the laws, rules, and regulations of the Church of God in Christ
2. Misfeasance, malfeasance, or nonfeasance in office
3. Conviction of a felony or misdemeanor involving moral turpitude in a court of law
4. Espousing doctrines repugnant to the articles of faith of the Church of God in Christ
5. Personal misconduct
6. Misappropriation or misuse of the funds of the church
7. Conduct unbecoming of a minister of the gospel

HANDOUT NO. 8

COULD YOU JUST LISTEN

WHEN I ASK you to listen to me and you start giving me advice, you have not done what I asked.

When I ask you to listen to me and you begin to tell me why I shouldn't feel that way, you are trampling on my feelings.

When I ask you to listen to me and you feel you have to do something to solve my problem, you have failed me, strange as that may seem.

Listen! All I asked was that you listen, not talk or do—just hear me.

Advice is cheap. Twenty cents will get you both Dear Abby and Billy Graham in the same paper.

I can do for myself; I am not helpless—maybe discouraged and faltering, but not helpless.

When you do something for me that I can and need to do for myself, you contribute to my fear and inadequacy.

But when you accept the simple fact that I do feel what I feel, no matter how irrational, then I can quit trying to convince you and get about this business of understanding what's behind this irrational feeling. When that's clear, the answers are obvious and I don't need advice.

Irrational feelings make more sense when we understand what's behind them.

Perhaps that's why prayer works, sometimes, for some people—because God is mute, and he/she doesn't give advice or try to fix things. "They" just listen, and you work it out for yourself.

So please listen and just hear me.

And if you want to talk, wait a minute for your turn—and I will listen to you.

HANDOUT NO. 9

Thomas J. Jackson Sr. Memorial District Superintendent Thomas Jackson Jr. Organizing A New Church

ONE IDEA OF *church* in the New Testament, which we shall consider here for this specific purpose, was "a community gathered by God through Christ." The church belongs to God because he has called it into being, dwells within it, rules over it, and realizes his purpose through it.

A real, true church conforms to God's Word; thus, it must follow in doctrine, character, organization, and practice the direction given it by the Bible.

Proverbs 29:18 states, "Where there is no vision, the people perish." Therefore, before organizing a new church, one must seek a vision and direction from God; then armed with what has been given and divinely inspired by God, a person can proceed with organization.

Procedure in Organizing a New Church

After praying, meditating, and seeking God's direction for what you believe to be the direction of the Holy Spirit, and after receiving the assurance and the vision, the following is a suggested method for getting started:

I. Call a meeting of family, baptized believers, and all that are interested in organizing a church.
II. At this meeting, discuss the purpose for organizing a new church; then codify and adopt the same into a resolution.

III. At this meeting (and subsequent meetings), there are several factors to be considered in organizing a new church. Each area is vitally important and must be given careful consideration.

    A. STRUCTURE: METHODOLOGY FOR A MEANINGFUL MINISTRY
1. Organization: identify church's role; set goals and objectives.
2. Personnel and staff requirements.
3. Corporate charter, constitution, bylaws (civil).
4. Site and facility, insurance.
5. IRS compliance and tax exemption.
6. Finance: ministry plan, financing plan, and spending plan.

    B. SPIRITUAL MINISTRY
1. Worship (service format)
2. Ministry plan: organizing committee
3. Education (all ages)
4. Fellowship (among members)

    C. DISCIPLESHIP
1. Stewardship (of abilities and financial gifts)
2. Lay leadership development
3. Outreach and evangelism
4. Social ministries
   a. Family needs
   b. Services
   c. Relationships: COGIC, community, businesses, other churches

IV. Remember that the church is the body of Christ, a living organism, and that it evangelizes and witnesses through its members, energizing people with the Holy Spirit so that they may be transformed into dynamic individuals, ministering in a changing global environment.

INDEX

A

active listening
  encouraging behavior, 47
Adam, 39
angel, Bible passages on, 40
anger, 30
appellate court, 11, 138, 141
arrogance, 21
atonement, 17
attitude, 19, 24
  defeatist, vii
audience, 18
authority, parliamentary, 51, 93

B

baptism, 17, 38–39, 42
believers, 32, 37–38, 40, 42, 161
Bible, 21–23, 32, 37, 40–41, 161
biblical principles, 58
bishop, presiding, 9–10, 68, 71, 75, 98
bishops, board of, 8–9, 16, 138, 141, 147
black community, 1
board, judiciary, 138–39, 141–48, 150

board member, judiciary, 144, 148
body, 25, 38, 45
body language, 45
budget, 97–98, 105–6, 110, 124, 129–30
  capital, 103–4
  consolidated jurisdictional, 99, 111, 121–22, 124
  consolidating jurisdictional, 99, 111, 119, 121, 124
  jurisdictional, 103–4, 113, 119, 122, 124
  preliminary, 110
  ministry meeting, 110
  operating, 103
budget calendar, 112–13, 121, 124
budget estimates, 110
budget plan, jurisdictional, 97
budget request, annual, 146
budget summary, 111, 122
bylaws, 5, 33, 50–51, 84, 162

C

Caesarea Philippi, 40
calmness, 25
campaigning, 60

certificates, 70, 80–81, 86, 145
chairman, 80, 83, 93, 143, 145, 148
   legislative branch headed by, 10
   trial of a, 148
chaplain, 80
character, 26
   developing a strong, 25
   elements of a good, 25
   fear and, 27
   how one can achieve, 27
   how to develop a good, 27
charter, 5, 50–51
check, jurisdictional, 129
church, 1, 32–33, 40, 78, 90, 161
   local, 63–64, 73–74, 76–78, 84–88, 90
   ordinances of, 41
church government, 7, 138–39
   three branches of, 10
church law, 11
Church of God in Christ, 7, 68
   constitution overview of, 7–9
   divine healing in, 41
   doctrines of, 91
   miracles in, 41
   mission statement of, 65
   ordinances of, 41
   three branches of, 10
civil officers, 70
clear thinking, 25–27, 29–30
clerk, 88, 91, 156. *See also* secretary
Coffey, Lillian Brooks, 68
committee
   investigating, 63, 74, 88–89, 91, 145, 154, 156

jurisdictional budget, 109–13, 121, 124, 129–30
common sense, 26, 30, 49
communication, nonverbal, 45
community, 32–33, 59–60, 161
compassion, 21
competition, 19
complacency, vii
conduct, 21, 90, 148, 158
conversations, social, 43
conversion, vii, 38–39
council, ecclesiastical, 83, 89
council of pastors and elders, 83, 139, 141, 143, 147, 155
counsel, 89, 91, 153, 156
   chief, 146
Creation, 37, 40
credentials, 8, 81, 86, 143, 146
credentials committee, 81

D

death of Christ, 17, 41–42
decision, majority, 89
delegate, 12, 73, 79, 81, 83, 144
delegates, certification of, 12, 80
demoniac beings. *See* devils
demons
   Bible passages on, 40
department heads, 73, 79
devils, 22, 40. *See also* Satan
diligence, 60
directors, board of, 7, 70, 78, 109–10, 125
disciples, 41

discipleship, 33
district assembly, 73
districts, 72
divine call, 22
divine healing, 41
doctrines, 17, 32, 37, 77, 79, 84, 161
dress, 45

E

earth, 17, 40
education, 33
"ekklesia". *See* church
elder, 147
election process, 9, 12
electorate, 12
emotion, 27
evangelism, vii, 33
   department of, 78, 93
executive branch, v, 7, 10, 138
executive clemency, 146
Executive Leadership Institute, vi
expenses, 85, 130
   total budgeted, 124
eye contact, 45

F

failure, 20–22
faith, 18, 39–42
   articles of, 8, 82, 88, 90
   Bible passages on, 39
   declaration of, 68
Father, 37–38, 42
fear, 27–30, 159

feet washing, 3, 17, 42
fellowship, 17, 33
finance, 33, 63, 74, 104
financing plan, 33, 104
forbidden fruit, 39
Ford, Louis Henry, 68
form
   cash receipts report, 129
   check request, 129, 134
   expenditure reimbursement, 129, 133
   expenditure requisition, 129–30
   requisition, 129, 134

G

general assembly, 8–12, 16, 69, 72–73, 80, 85, 138, 141–48
general board, 9, 16, 75, 138, 141, 146–47
general council, 16, 92, 141, 155, 157
general secretary, 12, 84, 87–88, 90–91, 145, 148, 156
glory, 38, 40
God's power, 22
GOOD, 4
good standing, 83
Gospel, 37, 39
Great Commission
   Bible passages on, 65, 67

H

harmony, 25, 49, 51
healing, 18, 41, 65, 67

heaven, 37, 40
holiness, 39
Holy Communion, 3, 17, 41
Holy Scripture, 68
Holy Spirit (Holy Ghost), 32–33, 38–39, 41–42
home and foreign missions, department of, 78
humility, 17, 42
humor, 46

I

imagination, 27, 29–30
immersion, 42
impulsiveness, 25
incidental motions, 52, 54
irritability, 25

J

James, 41
Jesus, 22, 37–41, 79, 84
judicial branch, 7, 11, 138
judicial code, 145
judiciary qualifications and nominations, 142–43
jurisdiction, ecclesiastical, 71–72, 74, 84, 86, 90–91
jurisdictional assemblies, 69
jurisdictional bishop, 12, 16, 71, 73, 75, 77, 80–81, 83–84, 86–92, 111–12, 139, 141, 145–46, 153–54, 156
jurisdictional budget summary, consolidated, 111, 122, 124

L

law, parliamentary, 49–51
lay delegate, 73, 79
leaders, Christian, vii
leadership, 8, 59, 68–69, 72, 98
   positive, 1
legislative branch, v, 7, 10, 138
logic, 25–27, 29–30, 49
Lord's Supper, 17, 41–42
love, 42, 68

M

main motions, 52–54
malfeasance, 90
meditation, 4, 19–20
memorial, 17
message, 18
ministers, i, 1
ministry, pastoral, 71
ministry plan, 33, 58–59, 104–7, 109–11, 113
miracle, 41
misconduct, 90, 158
misfeasance, 90
missionary, 76–77
   district, 12, 73, 75, 81
moral turpitude, 90, 158
motions, 52–55
muscles, 45
Music Department, 93, 125

N

National General Assembly, 69
National General Council, 157
national headquarters, 85, 91
national officers, 16, 147
negativism, vii
New Testament, 32, 37, 40, 68, 161
nominating committee, 143
nonfeasance, 90

O

offenses, 88, 90–91, 157–58
office, pastoral, 20
officer, chief executive, 10, 71, 82, 84
officers, jurisdictional, 75, 92
Old Testament, 37, 40
ordinances, 3, 41–42, 86
ordination committee, 86
original sin, 39
outreach, 33, 72

P

parliamentarian, 80
parliamentary law. *See* law, parliamentary
parliamentary procedure. *See* procedure, parliamentary
parliamentary rules. *See* rules, parliamentary
passion, 27, 30
pastor, 20, 22, 86–87
   appeal of, 92, 147, 155, 157
   disputes between members and, 63, 74
   failure of, 20–21
   local, 63, 73, 75, 90, 156
   of local churches, 84
   prayer and, 21–22
   success of, 22
   suspension of, 91
   trial of, 90–91, 156, 158
   vision and, 23
pastoral burnout, 59
pastoral office
   importance of, 20
   responsibilities, 20
pastorate, 20–21, 86
patience, 24–25
Paul (apostle), 38
Pauline Epistles, 40
performance report, 99, 130
personality, 18–19
personal property, 85
Peter (apostle), 40
petitioner, 145
petty-cash fund, 99, 130, 135
power, 40–41, 49
prayer, 20–22, 41, 160
preacher, 3, 21
preaching, 18, 20
preamble, 9, 68
preparation, 20–21, 72, 113
   budget, 109, 111
president, 7, 70, 77–78
presiding bishop, 9–10, 71, 75
principal parties, 89, 91, 145, 156
privileged motions, 52–53

problem solving, 1
procedure, parliamentary, 49–51
purpose, vii, 25, 32

R

reason, 25–26
reasoning, 26–27, 29–30
redemption, 39
regeneration, 39, 42
religion, articles of, 3
repentance, 17, 39
reputation, 25
resolution, 7, 32, 69, 138–39, 161
responsibility, male, 1
revenues, 118–19, 124
   total budgeted, 124
review committee, judicial, 154
righteousness, 40–41
Roberts, William Matthew, 68
role identification, 1
rules, parliamentary, 50–51

S

sacrament, 17
sacrifice, 17
salvation, 39, 42
sanctification, 38–39
   Bible passages on, 39
Satan, 28, 40. *See also* devils
scriptures, vii, 20, 37
Second Coming
   Bible passages on, 40

secretary, 7–9, 12, 66, 69–70, 78, 80–81, 83–84, 86–93, 141–45, 147–48, 156
   jurisdictional, 80–81, 86–87, 89
secretary of state, 7–9
secret ballot, 87
sergeant at arms, 80
services, 1, 20, 33, 38, 42, 76, 80, 118, 123
Shelby County Chancery Court, 8
sick, 20, 41
sin, 17, 21, 37–39
soul, 22, 30, 38–39, 42
spending plan, 33, 104
spring conference, annual. *See* workers' meeting
stewardship, 33, 162
subsidiary motions, 52–53
success, 3, 21–23, 60
suffering servant
   Bible passages on, 38
Sunday school, 77, 92
Sunday school department, 77
superintendent
   district, 63, 73–76, 81, 147, 161
   jurisdictional, 77
supervisor, jurisdictional, vi, 12, 74–75, 77, 81
supreme court. *See* judiciary board
sympathy, 21

T

thoughts, impulsive, 25
three-branch system, 138

treasurer, 7, 70, 78, 83, 129, 131
trial, 8, 83, 88–92, 145, 147–48, 153–54, 156
triangular plan, 105
Trinity (Triune Godhead), 37–38
trustees, 8, 85–86, 90
  board of, 146
truth, 18, 38–41
twenty-first century, 2, 12

U

unsaved, 20
unwillingness, vii
Usher Department, 93

V

vice president, first, 70
Virgin Birth, 37
vision, vi–vii, 21, 23–24, 58–60, 98
  Bible passage on, 32, 161
"visioneering," 58
vision goals, 60
vision plan, 59
voice, tone of, 45
vote, majority, 51, 81, 91–93, 146, 154, 157

W

water baptism, 42
weaknesses, 19, 27, 152
will of God, 40
wisdom, 1, 20–21, 40

women's work, 12, 75
Word of God, 22, 32, 37, 41, 161
work, vii, ix, 12, 19–20, 22, 31, 39, 59, 63, 65, 74–78, 154, 160
workers' meeting, 72, 92, 125
worship, 33

Y

Young People's Department, 77–78
Young People's Willing Workers, 77–78